Getting Textbooks to Every Child
in Sub-Saharan Africa

DIRECTIONS IN DEVELOPMENT
Human Development

Getting Textbooks to Every Child in Sub-Saharan Africa

Strategies for Addressing the High Cost and Low Availability Problem

Birger Fredriksen and Sukhdeep Brar
with Michael Trucano

© 2015 International Bank for Reconstruction and Development / The World Bank
1818 H Street NW, Washington, DC 20433
Telephone: 202-473-1000; Internet: www.worldbank.org

Some rights reserved

1 2 3 4   18 17 16 15

This work is a product of the staff of The World Bank with external contributions. The findings, interpretations, and conclusions expressed in this work do not necessarily reflect the views of The World Bank, its Board of Executive Directors, or the governments they represent. The World Bank does not guarantee the accuracy of the data included in this work. The boundaries, colors, denominations, and other information shown on any map in this work do not imply any judgment on the part of The World Bank concerning the legal status of any territory or the endorsement or acceptance of such boundaries.

Nothing herein shall constitute or be considered to be a limitation upon or waiver of the privileges and immunities of The World Bank, all of which are specifically reserved.

Rights and Permissions

This work is available under the Creative Commons Attribution 3.0 IGO license (CC BY 3.0 IGO) http://creativecommons.org/licenses/by/3.0/igo. Under the Creative Commons Attribution license, you are free to copy, distribute, transmit, and adapt this work, including for commercial purposes, under the following conditions:

Attribution—Please cite the work as follows: Fredriksen, Birger, and Sukhdeep Brar, with Michael Trucano. 2015. *Getting Textbooks to Every Child in Sub-Saharan Africa: Strategies for Addressing the High Cost and Low Availability Problem*. Directions in Development. Washington, DC: World Bank. doi: 10.1596/978-1-4648-0540-0. License: Creative Commons Attribution CC BY 3.0 IGO

Translations—If you create a translation of this work, please add the following disclaimer along with the attribution: *This translation was not created by The World Bank and should not be considered an official World Bank translation. The World Bank shall not be liable for any content or error in this translation.*

Adaptations—If you create an adaptation of this work, please add the following disclaimer along with the attribution: *This is an adaptation of an original work by The World Bank. Views and opinions expressed in the adaptation are the sole responsibility of the author or authors of the adaptation and are not endorsed by The World Bank.*

Third-party content—The World Bank does not necessarily own each component of the content contained within the work. The World Bank therefore does not warrant that the use of any third-party-owned individual component or part contained in the work will not infringe on the rights of those third parties. The risk of claims resulting from such infringement rests solely with you. If you wish to re-use a component of the work, it is your responsibility to determine whether permission is needed for that re-use and to obtain permission from the copyright owner. Examples of components can include, but are not limited to, tables, figures, or images.

All queries on rights and licenses should be addressed to the Publishing and Knowledge Division, The World Bank, 1818 H Street NW, Washington, DC 20433, USA; fax: 202-522-2625; e-mail: pubrights@worldbank.org.

ISBN (paper): 978-1-4648-0540-0
ISBN (electronic): 978-1-4648-0541-7
DOI: 10.1596/978-1-4648-0540-0

Cover photo: © Peter Darvas. Used with the permission of Peter Darvas. Further permission required for reuse.

Library of Congress Cataloging-in-Publication Data has been requested.

Contents

Foreword ix
Acknowledgments xi
About the Authors xiii
Abbreviations xv

	Executive Summary	1
	Objective of the Study	1
	Main Findings	2
	Notes	8
	References	8
Chapter 1	**Introduction and Rationale for This Study**	9
	Notes	12
	References	13
Chapter 2	**The State of Textbook Provision in Sub-Saharan Africa**	15
	Note	17
	References	17
Chapter 3	**Factors Contributing to Textbook Scarcity**	19
	Note	20
	Reference	20
Chapter 4	**The Urgency of Addressing the Textbook Shortage in Sub-Saharan Africa**	21
	Notes	26
	References	26
Chapter 5	**Factors Determining Textbook Costs**	29
	Unit Textbook Costs	31
	Annualized per-Student Textbook Costs	44
	Actual Unit and Annualized Textbook Costs in SSA	46
	Interventions and Scope for Reducing Textbook Costs	48

	Notes	50
	References	51
Chapter 6	**Textbook Financing**	**53**
	Issues	53
	Sources and Methods of Textbook Funding in SSA	54
	Government Textbook Funding in SSA	56
	Estimated Share of Primary Education Budget Needed for Adequate Supply of Textbooks	60
	Estimated Share of Secondary Education Budget Needed for Adequate Supply of Textbooks	65
	Impact of External Aid	71
	Notes	73
	References	74
Chapter 7	**Lessons for Sub-Saharan Africa from Countries in Other Regions**	**77**
	India	77
	The Philippines	79
	Vietnam	81
	Summary	83
	Notes	84
	References	84
Chapter 8	**Digital Teaching and Learning Materials: Opportunities, Options, and Issues**	**85**
	Predictions about the Demise of Printed Textbooks	85
	Educational Materials and Electronic Devices: Promise and Potential	85
	Some Common Myths and Misconceptions	86
	Costs	88
	One Way to Begin: Targeting Different Age Groups or School Subjects	91
	General Trends	92
	The Way Forward: Some Questions and Issues for Consideration	93
	Ten Recommendations for Policymakers	97
	Notes	99
	References	100
Chapter 9	**Lessons and Recommendations**	**101**
	How Can Sub-Saharan Countries Lower the High Costs of Providing Textbooks?	102
	References	106

Box

5.1	Evolution of Textbook Publishing in Sub-Saharan Africa	33

Figures

4.1	Percentage of Grade 6 Students Reaching SACMEQ Skill Levels for Reading, 2007	22
5.1	Long Print Run Cost-Benefit Curve	39

Tables

2.1	Variations in Book:Pupil Ratios in Primary Education	16
5.1	Two Examples of Retail Price Cost Components of Commercially Sold Textbooks in SSA (%)	30
5.2	Textbook Price Components for State Publishers	32
5.3	Sources of Authorship, Publishing, Manufacturing, and Raw Materials for Grades 1, 6, 8, and 11	35
5.4	Comparative Prices for One- and Four-Year Textbook Specifications	37
5.5	Unit, System, and Annualized per-Student Costs for Grade 1, Selected Countries	46
5.6	Average Unit Price, Number of Books, and Cost of Textbook Set for Grade 9, 2007, Selected Countries	48
6.1	Sources of Textbook Funding	55
6.2	Share of Total Recurrent Public Education Budgets for Primary and Secondary Education Spent on TLM, 2009 or Most Recent Year (%)	59
6.3	Estimated Share of Primary Education Budget (Recurrent and Capital) Needed to Provide Textbooks for Different Unit and System Costs	61
6.4	Annual Textbook Costs per Primary School Pupil for Different Unit and System Costs (US$)	62
6.5	Share of Primary Education Budget Needed to Provide Textbooks for Different Unit and System Costs (%)	63
6.6	Cost of Teaching and Learning Materials Other than Textbooks	64
6.7	Estimated Share of Secondary Education Budget (Recurrent and Capital) Needed to Provide Textbooks for Different Unit and System Costs	66
6.8	Annual Textbook Costs per Secondary School Student for Different Unit and System Costs (US$)	67
6.9	Share of Secondary Education Budget Needed to Provide Students with Textbooks for Different Unit and System Costs (%)	68
6.10	Annual per-Student Book Costs and Budget Shares to Provide Students with Textbooks for Different Unit and System Costs in Secondary Education, Total and by Cycle	69

7.1	India: Cost of Textbooks per Pupil and Set of Textbooks by Grade, 2011	79
7.2	The Philippines: Cost of Textbooks per Pupil per Set of Textbooks by Grade	81
7.3	Vietnam: Cost of Textbooks per Pupil per Set of Textbooks by Grade	82

Foreword

Even as African countries work toward achieving better learning outcomes for children through systemic reform, the affordability and availability of textbooks remains a persistent challenge across the continent. Although development partners, including the World Bank Group, have provided extensive technical support and funding for textbooks, shortages continue to hamper learning. While textbooks are not the only factor influencing student learning outcomes, their unavailability deprives students of an additional learning resource and of the opportunity to develop good reading habits. The lack of textbooks also deprives teachers of much-needed teaching support. The scale of the problem is worsened because of rapid student population growth. The supply of textbooks is simply unable to keep up with demand, and costs can be prohibitive for low-income families.

This study aims to generate discussion among policy makers, development partners, and other stakeholders in Africa on the policy options that can help reduce textbook costs and increase their supply. It explores, in depth, the cost and financial barriers that restrict textbook availability in schools across much of the region. It also examines policies adopted in India, the Philippines, and Vietnam that have helped these countries make textbooks affordable and available for all children. Finally, the study provides a thorough assessment of the pros and cons of digital teaching and learning materials and cautions against the assumption that they can immediately replace printed textbooks. On a personal basis, as secretary of education of Rio de Janeiro, I found it helpful to have both: textbooks and digital classes, including online reading materials, such as e-books.

The breadth of information and analysis in the study is both practical and relevant, because there is no quick fix to the mounting problem of textbook scarcity. To achieve the goal of each child having access to textbooks, countries need to make well-informed policy choices within the prevailing country context. These choices then need to be supported by a time-bound action plan for methodical capacity building within national education systems as well as by strategic partnerships with the private sector to ensure that the teaching and learning materials are designed to support student learning and can be produced at costs that make them widely available. While good policies can ensure sustained funding and improved efficiency and reverse the damage done by decades of textbook scarcity, school managements will also have to rise to the challenge of storing and equitably distributing textbooks.

Despite the complexity of the factors affecting textbook provision, the study's recommendations are simple and lay out clearly the short- and longer-term options available to policy makers. Ultimately, the goal of affordable books for all children in Sub-Saharan Africa is within reach, and rapid incremental improvement in this area, alongside other systemic reforms, will help raise education outcomes across the region.

Claudia Maria Costin
Senior Director, Education Global Practice
World Bank Group

Acknowledgments

This report is a product of collaboration between its principal authors, Birger Fredriksen and Sukhdeep Brar. The report draws heavily from a complementary report, *Where Have All the Textbooks Gone: The Affordable and Sustainable Provision of Teaching and Learning Materials In Sub-Saharan Africa* (Washington, DC: World Bank, forthcoming), prepared by Tony Read with inputs from Vincent Bontoux. The chapter on digital teaching and learning materials is contributed by Michael Trucano.

The report has also benefitted from feedback and review by a large number of colleagues. During the initial stages of the study, Christopher Thomas, Jee-Peng Tan, and Luis Benveniste provided valuable inputs into the scope and design of the study. It was peer-reviewed at different stages by Prema Clarke, Helen Craig, Helen Abdazi, Sakhevar Diop, Shwetlena Sabarwal, Harsha Aturupane, Reehana Raza, Shobhana Sosale, Adama Ouedraogo, and Pierre Kamano. Valuable inputs were also received from Nathalie Lahire and Richard Crabbe. Laura McDonald's help in managing internal processes is appreciated. Chandrani Raysarkar coordinated the overall publication process of the report. The authors would also like to thank Deon Filmer and Peter Materu for their guidance in finalizing the report.

This report was made possible by generous grants from the Norwegian Pre- and Post-Primary Education Trust Fund (NPEF) and the Multi-Donor Education and Skills Fund (MESF), which are gratefully acknowledged.

About the Authors

Birger Fredriksen is a consultant on education policies in developing countries and chairs the Governing Board of the International Institute for Educational Planning of the United Nations Educational, Scientific and Cultural Organization (UNESCO). Before retiring, he worked for 20 years at the World Bank including as director of human development for Africa, macroeconomic division chief for Western Africa, and division chief for human development in the Sahel Department. Prior to that, he was principal education planner in the Education and Employment Division, and education task team leader for most countries in the Sahel. Before joining the World Bank, Mr. Fredriksen established and headed for three years the Division of International Economics at the Norwegian Institute of Foreign Affairs, Oslo, Norway. He worked for ten years in various positions at UNESCO, Paris; for two years at the Organisation for Economic Co-operation and Development, Paris; and for two years at the University of Oslo. Mr. Fredriksen, a Norwegian, holds a master's degree in economics from the University of Oslo and a PhD on educational planning in developing countries from the University of Lancaster, U.K. Mr. Fredriksen has written extensively on education development, especially in Sub-Saharan Africa.

Sukhdeep Brar began her career with the Indian Administrative Service, India's premier civil service. She spent six years in the Ministry of Human Resource Development, Department of Education, New Delhi, where she administered several national programs and was instrumental in designing a program for computer education through public-private partnerships that was adopted in 1992 for nationwide implementation in public secondary schools in India. She also served as Economic Counselor in the Embassy of India in Washington, DC, with responsibility for liaison on economic policy with the U.S. government and promoting investment in India. Ms. Brar, a senior education specialist, has been with the World Bank since January 2009. She was based in Uganda until January 2013 where she managed the Bank's education portfolio. Prior to joining the World Bank, she was Principal Education Specialist with the Asian Development Bank based in Manila, the Philippines. Ms. Brar has worked in India, Nepal, Sri Lanka, Bangladesh, Vietnam, Lao People's Democratic Republic, Cambodia, Malaysia, Uganda, Tanzania, Ghana, and Nigeria. Ms. Brar holds two master's degrees from Cornell University.

Michael Trucano is the World Bank's senior specialist for information and communication techology (ICT) and education policy. He serves as the focal point on use of technology in education around the world, and on ICT use for development (ICT4D). He provides policy advice and technical assistance to governments seeking to apply new ICTs in their education systems. He is the principal voice behind the Bank's EduTech blog. Mr. Trucano leads the World Bank's related analytical work under its flagship Systems Approach for Better Education Results initiative as it relates to ICTs (SABER-ICT). Mr. Trucano previously served as the ICT and education specialist at infoDev, the multi-donor "ICT knowledge shop" housed within the World Bank's Global ICT Department (GICT), where he coordinated activities related to ICTs and the Millennium Development Goals ("ICTs for MDGs"), especially as they related to education. Mr. Trucano joined the World Bank Group in 1997, initially with the International Finance Corporation and later with the World Bank Institute, where he was a core member of the team that developed the World Links for Development Program.

Abbreviations

CMS	content management system
CUE	Center for Universal Education
EFA	Education for All
FOB	free on board
GDP	gross domestic product
GER	gross enrollment ratio
GNP	gross national product
ICTs	information and communication technologies
IDA	International Development Association
IP	intellectual property
LMS	learning management system
MOET	Ministry of Education and Training
NCERT	National Council of Education Research and Training
OER	Open Education Resources
PASEC	Program on the Analysis of Education Systems
SACMEQ	Southern and Eastern Africa Consortium for Monitoring Education Quality
SSA	Sub-Saharan Africa
TLM	teaching and learning materials
UIS	UNESCO Institute of Statistics

Executive Summary

This study is part of the World Bank Group's long-standing efforts to help countries in Sub-Saharan Africa (SSA) provide adequate, effective teaching and learning materials (TLM) to all of their students in primary and secondary schools. Since the 1980s the Bank has consistently emphasized—through its analytical work, policy advice, and lending—that achieving this goal is often the most cost-effective way of improving learning outcomes. That is especially the case in SSA given the key role that such materials play in compensating for shortages of other high-quality education inputs.

The World Bank's (1988) first SSA-specific education policy paper emphasized that providing a minimum package of TLM to *all students* would be essential to improving the quality of learning, including by enhancing the productive use of the two most costly education inputs: teachers' and students' time. The next SSA-specific education policy paper (World Bank 2001) reiterated this message. However, as noted in that paper, as well as in two subsequent reviews of textbook issues in SSA (World Bank 2002, 2008), despite extensive technical support and funding from external partners, making textbooks affordable and available to all students remains an elusive objective for most countries.

Why has it been so hard to improve textbook provision? Improving the affordability and availability of textbooks should be an easy way to advance learning outcomes in SSA. Other regions have been able to do so; why not most Sub-Saharan countries? Many studies, including those mentioned above, have identified bottlenecks in each link of the "textbook chain"—development, manufacturing, procurement, financing, distribution, and effective use—causing the problems of high costs and low availability, and offered suggestions on how to remove them. This is an area of education reform where lack of knowledge about what to do is not the main constraint. Rather, progress has been hampered by limited capacity to translate that knowledge into actions tailored to addressing national constraints, and by weak political will to take those actions.

Objective of the Study

The objective of the study is to identify the cost and financing constraints to text book provision and thereby help countries remove constraints on timely provision of affordable textbooks to all students in *primary and secondary education*.

To this end, the study focuses exclusively on cost and financing barriers and does not seek to examine other issues associated with textbook provision such as logistics of textbook provision (textbook development, procurement, distribution, storage, etc.), their use in the classroom, or their impact on learning outcomes.

To set the stage, the study starts by highlighting textbook availability (chapter 2), summarizes the factors causing textbook scarcity (chapter 3), and reiterates the urgency of addressing the shortages (chapter 4).[1] However, unlike most studies that addressed textbook availability, this study focuses on *textbook cost* (chapter 5) and *financing issues* (chapter 6), in an effort to address two questions. First, what is the *actual* cost of textbooks in the region, and *how much scope is there for lowering these costs*?[2] Second, what share of education budgets do countries *actually* allocate to TLM, and what shares would be needed to meet national targets in systems that have achieved affordable *unit* and *system* textbook costs? To provide a comparative perspective, chapter 7 discusses experiences with textbook provision in India, the Philippines, and Vietnam. Chapter 8 explores the opportunities offered by digital TLM. Chapter 9 concludes with lessons and recommendations. The study draws heavily on extensive background work undertaken to inform the analysis, conclusions, and recommendations.[3]

Main Findings

Severe shortages of comparable data make it difficult to assess why textbooks cost so much and are in such short supply in SSA. For example, it is often difficult to know whether data on *textbook availability* refer to targets or to actual availability, whether textbooks available at schools are available to and effectively used by students, and whether *unit textbook cost* refers to just *manufacturing costs* (largely paper and printing) or *retail price* or something in between. The last point is particularly important because manufacturing costs often account for just one-third of retail prices. Moreover, data on financing often cover, at best, public financing—leaving out major sources such as donors and parents.

Insufficient financing is the main and most common constraint, though not the only constraint on textbook availability across countries. Factors impacting high textbook costs vary widely between countries depending on issues such as local publishing capacity, the roles of the public and private sectors in the textbook chain, languages of instruction, policies on textbook choices, and financing modes—including the role and predictability of external funding and textbook distribution and storage capacity.

Insufficient financing need not be a binding constraint. Systems could be put in place to address the factors causing unaffordable prices and unpredictable financing. Other issues that directly affect textbook costs are relevant to most SSA countries. But policies and actions need to be country-specific; there is no blue print. National systems for textbook provision are weak in most countries in the region. These include developing systems for annual monitoring of textbook needs to cater to enrollment growth and book replacement; identifying, developing, and implementing actions to reduce textbook unit, system, and distribution costs; and ensuring predictable annual financing.

Textbook Availability

Most SSA countries face severe book shortages even in core subjects. A survey of 22 SSA countries found that, in 2010, the "median country" had 1.4 students per textbook in both reading and math in primary education—ranging from less than one pupil per book to 11 for reading and 13 for math.[4] A 2008 study for secondary education found that 18 of 19 SSA countries surveyed suffered from a severe shortage of books for most students. The availability was best for language and math, but very poor in non-core subjects (eight students per book in the best case). And availability is much poorer in rural areas: less than 5 percent of rural students had access to books even in core subjects.

The level of scarcity does not appear to have improved much in recent decades. The stagnation of education budgets in the 1980s and early 1990s led to declines in public spending per pupil, resulting in school fees, the need for parents to buy textbooks, or both. The trend toward abolishing fees since about 2000 and increasing education budgets (largely generated by economic growth but also by increased priority to education in domestic budgets and rise in external aid) increased textbook funding. But few countries managed to catch up with past backlog *and* respond to the sharp increases in enrollments.

The Urgency of Action

Shortages of TLM undermine better learning. A range of studies concur that learning outcomes are weak in SSA, and the remarkable increase in access since 2000 has not been matched by comparable progress in learning outcomes. Given growing global awareness that actual learning—not just years of schooling—is the key determinant of the benefits that education offers to individuals and nations, there is an increased urgency for SSA countries to deal with the factors that constrain students' opportunities to learn. Over the past several decades, several studies have concluded that investments in TLM would likely have had a greater impact on student achievements than investing the same amount of resources in other education inputs. Thus, it is time for Sub-Saharan African countries to address their problems with the high costs and low availability of textbooks.

Key Drivers of Textbook Unit Costs

In SSA countries, the following factors impact the retail price of *commercially produced books* at different stages of textbook production:

1. **Production costs** account for about one-third of retail price. That includes prepress work, paper and other raw materials, printing and binding. This further breaks down into 14 percent for origination, 12 percent for raw materials, and 10 percent for printing and binding.
2. **Publishers' overhead, marketing, and profit** account for about a quarter.

3. **Booksellers' discounts** also take about a quarter. This only applies if the books are supplied through the retail book trade; if they are supplied to the ministries of education, distribution costs are lower to the publisher and higher for the ministries.
4. **Distribution costs** account for about a tenth, depending on the role of the publishers, booksellers, and ministries of education in distribution.
5. **Authors' royalties** also account for about a tenth.

In the case of *state publishing*, costs under points 2, 3, 4, and 5 are often subsumed under the budget of various agencies of the ministries of education. Therefore, in this case, the unit costs reported refer mainly to production costs. This difference in coverage is often the *main factor* explaining the large differences in unit textbook cost reported by countries. Thus, production cost—the cost component that often gets most attention—*may not be the one offering the greatest scope for cost savings*, given that it only accounts for about one-third of retail price.

The *length of print runs* is a key determinant of unit production costs. The impact of this factor is sensitive to the number of colors used. For a four-color book, most of the economies of scale are gained at around 50,000 copies (half the unit cost of printing 5,000 copies). For a one-color book, the same magnitude of economies of scale is gained at print runs as low as 7,500—10,000 copies.

In the past, *poor governance and ineffective procurement* have been major factors causing high textbook costs. Addressing these factors often results in substantial price reduction. One way is to use the private sector for textbook publishing and distribution, an approach used by a growing number of countries. Using textbook price and minimum physical production specifications as key factors in textbook evaluation and contracting has also proven to be effective in both reducing price and enhancing quality.

In addition to unit cost, the *annual per pupil* textbook cost is determined by three key *system-related costs*: (a) The number of books needed in a specific grade, (b) the number of pupils per book, and (c) average book life. *System costs* are often more important in determining *annual per pupil costs* than unit costs. Despite this, countries generally do not take these costs into account when making decisions on the number of subjects covered in the curriculum, curriculum revisions necessitating new textbooks, and quality of warehousing and distribution systems to reduce the often very high levels of textbook damage and loss that reduce book life.

Actual and "Reasonable" Textbook Cost

Data from nine SSA countries show large variations in actual unit textbook costs both within and between grades. For example, in grade 1, unit costs ranged from US$0.75 to US$7.50. In grade 12, the variations were even greater, ranging from US$1.00 to US$15.00. In comparison, corresponding average unit costs of textbooks in India were US$0.67 at the primary level and US$5.31 at the secondary level. In the Philippines, the corresponding range was US$0.92–$1.10 and in Vietnam the range was US$0.70–$1.30. There were similar variations in system costs: The *median* targets for system cost factors at grade 1 were four books needed for the grade, one pupil per book, and 2.5 years average book life. The *median* targets for system cost factors were eight books needed for the grade, one pupil per book, and five years average book life.

Funding for Textbooks

The paucity of comparable data that bedevils the analysis of textbook availability and cost is even worse for textbook funding. There are three main sources of textbook funding in SSA: governments, parents, and external partners. Their relative importance varies widely between countries, over time, and by education level. And though donors continue to play a major role, it is difficult to quantify how much they fund and whether their funding is included in data on public education spending. In five of nine countries surveyed for this study, governments fund—through different approaches and often with heavy external support—the textbooks in primary education while parents pay for textbooks in secondary education.

Clearly, shortage of adequate and predictable funding is a constraint on the availability of textbooks. However, it is difficult to assess how *binding* this constraint is. For example, one major reason for shortage of funding is the high cost of textbooks. Therefore, unless the factors causing high prices are addressed, the financial resources are likely to remain constrained.

Based on the actual primary education budgets and enrollments for 31 SSA countries, we estimate that spending *3–4 percent* of this budget on textbooks would allow the "median" country to provide all pupils with five textbooks per grade, provided unit cost could be reduced to US$2.00 and average book life raised to three years. At that unit cost, the share could be reduced to about *2 percent* of education budgets if each pupil were provided with only three books and book life remains at three years. For the same unit cost, the budget share would have to increase to *10–11 percent* if each pupil were provided with five books and book life were only one year. To these amounts should be added at least 1–2 percent of the budget to provide a minimum package of other essential TLM.

Similarly, based on the actual secondary education budget and enrollments for 29 SSA countries, we estimate that spending *6–7 percent* of these budgets on textbooks would allow the "median country" to provide each pupil with five textbooks per grade if unit costs can be cut to US$5.00, and average book life were three years. For that unit cost, the share of education budgets could be reduced to about *4 percent* if each pupil had only five books and book life rose to five years. For the same unit cost, the budget share would need to increase to about *10 percent* if eight books were provided to each pupil and book life reduced to three years. The share of the budget needed for textbooks in the lower secondary cycle is more than twice that of the upper secondary cycle, mainly because public spending per pupil is on average more than twice as high in the upper cycle. Therefore, the costs of textbooks and their implications for textbook life are key to assessing textbook coverage and the costs that countries must incur to achieve it. Striking the right balance between cost and quality is crucial for sustained textbook provision.

It is difficult to compare textbook spending as a share of education budgets across countries. That holds for the Sub-Saharan African countries as well as India, the Philippines, and Vietnam. In India, the annual cost of free textbook provision for the entire school cycle is estimated to have been US$1.27 billion in 2010, or about 1.7 percent of public spending on education. In the Philippines, for the same year, providing textbooks on a 1:1 ratio of students to textbooks was US$63 million at the primary level and US$55 million at the secondary level. The Philippines, which depends heavily on external financing allocated 0.5 percent of its education budget to textbook provision in 2013. Vietnam does not make these figures public. But the share of spending on textbooks appears to be lower in these three countries compared to SSA because textbooks are less expensive.

Opportunities Offered by Electronic Teaching and Learning Materials

The landscape and potential for electronic learning are rapidly changing. Factors such as the rapid increase in quality and decline in prices of e-books and other electronic TLM, as well as the widespread availability of mobile phones, will radically change the options available in the future. Already there is a buzz about the potential for laptops, e-readers, and other information and communication technologies to overcome the shortcomings of strained school systems.

However, the choices are neither simple nor cost efficient, and there is no viable substitute for the traditional textbook in the near term. Moreover, it is unclear how the introduction of electronic TLM would affect financing needs. What is clear is that to harness the opportunities offered by electronic TLM, countries will need to put even more effort into dealing with issues related to all TLM, including the most cost-effective balances between different types of printed and electronic materials. Over the next decade, the most cost-effective approach will likely be a mix where printed materials continue to be used for certain subjects and electronic materials gradually replace school libraries, and are increasingly used especially for science teaching in secondary education, including by replacing traditional labs in some areas.

Experiences from Three Asian Countries

India, the Philippines, and Vietnam offer valuable lessons on where in the textbook chain cost savings could potentially be effected. They have had success in making textbooks affordable to the large majority of students, and because they are large and complex countries with diverse political and administrative systems. These three countries have ambitious policies and elaborate administrative and management structures for provision of textbooks that address many of the system weaknesses that are found in most SSA countries. Key aspects of the systems in these countries include:

- One standard textbook is provided for each subject. The textbooks are written to the curriculum.

- The number of textbooks required per grade is closer to the median for SSA in the Philippines, slightly higher in Vietnam, and lower in India.
- The government is responsible for content development, except in the Philippines where content development is contracted to private publishers.
- India and Vietnam retain full copyright, making reprinting cheaper. The Philippines retains right to reprint during the five-year cycle for procurement of books.
- Costs are managed in the case of Vietnam by using state printing houses and government procurement of large quantities of paper; in the case of India through competitive bidding among empaneled printers; and in the case of the Philippines by national competitive bidding but linking printing to content development.

Having achieved the ambitious targets of providing textbooks for all children, the three countries face the common challenge of improving the quality while keeping textbooks affordable and maintaining sustainable financing. In India, book life is one year since textbooks are distributed free of charge to all children each year. Thus, books are reprinted each year based on total reported enrollments. This seems inefficient since, in addition to distribution costs, the *annual* per pupil cost of a book lasting only one year is 2–3 times higher than one lasting four years. In Vietnam, the book life is reported to be four years; but since 60–70 percent of students buy their own books, this can only have meaning if the books are recirculated through an effective second-hand textbook market. In the Philippines, textbooks have a shelf life of five years and are made available to the students for the academic year, collected at the end of term and reissued to students the following year.

How Can Sub-Saharan Africa Lower the Costs and Increase the Availability of Textbooks?

Establish sustainable and transparent systems to:

- **Choose cost-effective teaching and learning material packages** when developing the curriculum and making evidence-based choices about textbooks, teachers' guides, school and/or class libraries and (increasingly) between written and electronic teaching learning materials.
- **Improve textbook procurement** by ensuring that price and production specifications are included in textbook evaluation and by using civil society organizations to help monitor textbook availability, quality, and costs.
- **Develop and implement cost reduction strategies** by reviewing the full scope for reducing the *total annual costs* of providing all pupils with the needed TLM.
- **Monitor each school's textbook availability and need** for annual replenishment and hold school managers accountable for effective textbook use and safe storage.
- **Ensure predictable and sustainable financing** for timely book procurement and delivery.

Given the complexity and involvement of the many constituencies, stakeholders, and vested interests, *implementation of the above type of strategy will require strong political will* to address the factors and interests preventing pupils from having affordable textbooks.

Notes

1. Parts of this study draw heavily on the findings of Read and Bontoux (forthcoming) that was commissioned to serve as a background study for this main study. This study is a draft of the recently finalized study referred to in footnote 3 below. It also draws upon three country comparator case studies, entitled *Making Textbooks Available to All students: Barriers and Options*, for India, the Philippines, and Vietnam, which are individually referenced in chapter 7.
2. As explained in chapter 5, this study uses three textbook cost concepts: (a) *Unit textbook cost*—retail price of one single textbook; (b) *System costs*—determined by the number of books needed in each grade, targeted book: student ratio, and average book life; and (c) *Annual per-student textbook cost*—i.e., the annual cost of providing one student with the textbooks needed in a specific grade for given unit and system costs.
3. First is Tony Read's *Where Have All the Textbooks Gone? The Affordable and Sustainable Provision of Learning and Teaching Materials in Sub-Saharan Africa*, with inputs on Francophone countries from Vincent Bontoux (Washington, DC: World Bank, forthcoming), a study that consolidates existing work on the subject but also includes country-specific data on textbook costs and provision specially collected for this work. Second are three studies on the provision of textbooks in the Philippines, Vietnam, and India—countries that have succeeded in providing low-cost textbooks affordable to all students.
4. The full references to the studies mentioned are given in the relevant sections of the main text.

References

Read, A., and V. Bontoux. Forthcoming. *Where Have All the Textbooks Gone? The Affordable and Sustainable Provision of Learning and Teaching Materials in Sub-Saharan Africa*. Washington, DC: World Bank.

World Bank. 1988. *Education in Sub-Saharan Africa: Policies for Adjustment, Revitalization, and Expansion*. A World Bank Study. Washington, DC: World Bank.

———. 2001. *A Chance to Learn: Knowledge and Finance for Education in Sub-Saharan Africa*. Africa Region Human Development Series. Washington, DC: World Bank.

———. 2002. "World Bank Support for Provision of Textbooks in Sub-Saharan Africa (1985–2000)." Africa Region Human Development Working Paper Series, World Bank, Washington, DC.

———. 2008. "Textbooks and School Library Provision in Secondary Education in Sub-Saharan Africa." Working Paper 126, Africa Region Human Development Working Paper Series, World Bank, Washington, DC.

CHAPTER 1

Introduction and Rationale for This Study

This study is part of the World Bank Group's long-standing efforts to help countries in Sub-Saharan Africa (SSA) provide adequate teaching and learning materials (TLM) to all students in primary and secondary school. Since the 1980s the Bank has consistently emphasized—through its analytical work, policy advice, and lending—that achieving this goal is perhaps the most cost-effective way of improving learning outcomes. For example, one of the main policy recommendations of the Bank's first SSA-specific education policy paper was that countries provide "a minimum package of textbooks and instructional materials," emphasizing that such materials are "critically" important if productive use is to be made of the two other (much more costly) inputs into education, namely, teachers' and students' time. The problem of inadequate supplies of books and materials "is especially acute (and relatively inexpensive to rectify) at the primary level, where an annual expenditure of about US$5 per pupil should meet minimum requirements" (World Bank 1988, 46).[1]

The Bank's next SSA-specific education policy paper reiterated the importance of TLM, arguing for "access to adequate textbooks and other learning materials for every child." But it also noted that "despite donor support, few countries have established financially and institutionally sustainable systems for book provision" (World Bank 2001, 36). In addition, since the early 2000s the Bank's Africa Region has conducted two extensive reviews of lessons learned in reaching the goal of textbooks for all students. The first (World Bank 2002) drew lessons from the Bank's support for textbooks in SSA during 1985–2000. The second (World Bank 2008) focused on the provision of textbooks and school libraries for secondary education. Based on the lessons from the Bank's extensive work on textbooks in SSA, both reports made detailed recommendations on how to move forward.[2]

In terms of education lending, over 1985–2000 the International Development Association (IDA, the Bank's lending facility for the poorest countries) funded 110 education projects in 40 SSA countries, of which 72 percent included support for textbooks.[3] Of these, 55 percent supported primary education only, 26 percent primary and secondary, and 6 percent secondary only. The rest covered tertiary only (7 percent) or a combination of the three levels (World Bank 2002, 5–8). Most other development agencies have given similarly high priority to TLM in their technical and financial assistance for education.

And, yet, *the majority of pupils in SSA still lack adequate access to textbooks*. The scarcity is even more acute for readers, teacher guides, school libraries, dictionaries, and other reference books. The elusiveness of progress in this area is alarming. There are several reasons for this.

- The importance of adequate provision of TLM is particularly important in SSA, given the role such materials play in compensating for the weakness of other quality inputs such as poorly trained teachers, high level of teacher absenteeism, large class size, short effective school year, high illiteracy among parents, and the shortage of reading materials at home.

- The target year of the 2015 Education for All (EFA) goals is upon us and progress toward the crucial "education quality goal" (EFA goal 6) has been particularly slow. As documented in successive (2007 and subsequent) *EFA Global Monitoring Reports*, average learning achievement levels in SSA countries are very low, and differences in learning levels are enormous between children from different population groups—and, in particular, between children from households at different income levels. Low learning achievements also put many SSA countries at risk of not achieving the Millennium Development Goal of universal completion of primary education.

- Since the EFA quality goal has not been achieved as of 2015, improving learning outcomes is a central component of the proposed post-2015 global education goals. In fact, the international community is giving sharply increasing attention to the quality of learning. This is needed both to enhance the learning achievements of all students and to reduce persistently high dropout rates: in 2009 only 71 percent of primary school students in SSA reached grade 5, a share that has changed little since the late 1970s. This new emphasis on learning is exemplified by the 2011 World Bank Education Strategy, which emphasizes that "getting value for the education dollar requires smart investments—that is, investments that have proven to contribute to learning. Quality has to be the focus of education investments, with learning gains as a metric of quality" (World Bank 2011, 4).[4] As summarized in chapter 2 of this study, research shows that investments in TLM are smart investments. But as shown by the persistent low availability of textbooks (see chapter 3), the considerable investments made so far, including with Bank support, have not achieved the target of adequate TLM for all pupils.

- Finally, studies have shown that learning levels—as measured by student scores on international assessments of literacy and math—are important in explaining differences between countries in economic growth, independent of differences in enrollment ratios (Hanusehek and Woessmann 2008). Failure to acquire requisite competences hampers a country's ability to develop the productive labor force required for knowledge- and technology-driven productivity growth. Furthermore, because low-quality education is much more common among poor and marginalized groups, failing to address the reasons for it (such as inadequate supply of TLM) undermines countries' opportunities to benefit from the redistributive effects of education. Ultimately, human capital through education is the *only capital* most very poor people can aspire to acquire.

Given the many reasons to address the factors behind weak learning outcomes, and the wide consensus that adequate provision of TLM is a key and cost-effective investment for improving learning, why has it been so difficult to ensure that all pupils have access to essential TLM? This seems like "low-hanging fruit" in the struggle to improve education quality, a fruit harvested long ago in most developing countries in other regions. Why does progress continue to elude so many SSA countries?

As already noted, many reports prepared over the years have identified the main constraints in each link of the "textbook chain"—development, manufacturing and publishing, procurement, financing, distribution, and effective use—and recommendations have been made on how to remove these constraints. *This is one of the many areas of education reform where lack of knowledge about what to do **is not** the key constraint on progress. Rather, the main challenges are translating that knowledge into national policies and action programs tailored to the national context and strengthening political will to implement those policies and programs.*

The main purpose of this study is to help support processes at the country level that have been designed to help countries achieve those challenges. Three key findings of the main background study (Read and Bontoux forthcoming) sponsored as part of this work program are as follows:

1. There are many factors causing the high textbook cost/low textbook availability problem faced by most SSA countries and the importance of each factor varies widely between countries. Therefore, *policies and actions to address them must be country-specific.* There is no blueprint that fits all countries.
2. One common cause across countries is the *weaknesses of the national systems* in the different links of the textbook chain to ensure timely, affordable provision of textbooks.
3. *Shortage of financing is one factor, but it need not be binding* if (a) systematic efforts are made to minimize annual per-student textbook costs by reducing textbook unit, system, and distribution costs, and (b) systems are put in place to ensure predictable financing for timely annual provision of new textbooks to cater to enrollment growth, replace textbooks, and reduce waste.

Based on these findings, this study focuses exclusively on the cost and financing side of the high cost/low availability problem. It does not examine other issues associated with textbook provision, such as logistics (development, procurement, distribution, storage, etc.), their use in classrooms, or their impact on learning outcomes. To set the stage, chapters 2, 3, and 4 summarize, respectively, data on textbook availability in SSA, the key factors causing textbook scarcity, and reasons for why addressing the textbook shortage is urgent. Chapter 5 provides the main discussion of cost and financing issues, summarizing the key cost-driving elements in each link of the textbook chain. Chapter 6 assesses the financial implications of achieving national targets for provision of textbooks. Together, chapters 5 and 6 aim to answer the following questions:

1. What is a reasonable retail price for a primary and secondary education textbook?
2. What share of the primary and secondary education budgets would countries need to devote to textbooks and other TLM to ensure adequate provision?

Chapter 7 discusses the experiences of countries in other regions. Chapter 8 explores the opportunities that the rapid developments and falling costs of electronic TLM offer for addressing the low availability/high-cost problem. Chapter 9 summarizes lessons and policy implications for SSA countries striving to ensure adequate availability of affordable textbooks.

Finally, as noted throughout this report, any comparative study of textbook availability, cost, and financing in SSA is complicated by the shortage of comparable data. For example, it is often difficult to know whether data on *textbook availability* refer to targets or to actual availability. The coverage of *cost data* varies widely, ranging from including just production costs or retail prices including all costs; retail prices can be three times production costs. And data on *financing* often at best cover just public financing, leaving out major sources such as donors and parents.

Notes

1. The paper estimated unit public expenditures per primary school student at US$48 (in 1983 US$; median for 33 SSA countries). Thus, US$5.00 per-student corresponds to about 10 percent of recurrent unit expenditures at that time. Chapter 6 of this report estimates the share of today's education budget that would need to be allocated to textbooks.
2. Beyond these Africa-specific textbook studies, the Bank has had a long-standing involvement in promoting textbooks in developing countries; see references throughout this study.
3. Prior to 1985, the first Bank-wide review of textbook support efforts found that 6 percent of Bank education projects had textbook components during 1965–72 and 32 percent during 1978–83.
4. The focus on learning is central to education strategies of other bilateral and multilateral development agencies as well. Also, institutions such as the Center for Universal Education (CUE) at Brookings, in cooperation with the UNESCO Institute of Statistics (UIS), have co-convened the Learning Matrix Task Force to help

"catalyze a shift in the global conversation on education from a focus on access to access plus learning. [T]he task force aims to make recommendations to help countries and international institutions measure and improve learning outcomes for children and youth worldwide" (CUE and UIS 2013, 1).

References

CUE and UIS (Center for Universal Education at Brookings and UNESCO Institute for Statistics). 2013. *Toward Universal Learning: What Every Child Should Learn*. Washington, DC: Brookings Institution.

Hanushek, E. A., and L. Woessmann. 2008. "The Role of Education Quality in Economic Growth." Policy Research Working Paper 4122, World Bank, Washington, DC.

Read, A., and V. Bontoux. Forthcoming. *Where Have All the Textbooks Gone? The Affordable and Sustainable Provision of Learning and Teaching Materials in Sub-Saharan Africa*. Washington, DC: World Bank.

UNESCO (United Nations Educational, Scientific, and Cultural Organization). 2007 (and subsequent years). *EFA Global Monitoring Report*. Paris: UNESCO.

World Bank. 1988. *Education in Sub-Saharan Africa: Policies for Adjustment, Revitalization, and Expansion*. A World Bank Study. Washington, DC: World Bank.

———. 2001. *A Chance to Learn: Knowledge and Finance for Education in Sub-Saharan Africa*. Africa Region Human Development Series. Washington, DC: World Bank.

———. 2002. "World Bank Support for Provision of Textbooks in Sub-Saharan Africa (1985–2000)." Africa Region Human Development Working Paper Series, World Bank, Washington, DC.

———. 2008. "Textbooks and School Library Provision in Secondary Education in Sub-Saharan Africa." Working Paper 126, Africa Region Human Development Working Paper Series, World Bank, Washington, DC.

———. 2011. *Learning for All: Investing in People's Knowledge and Skills to Promote Development—World Bank Group Education Strategy 2020*. Washington, DC: World Bank.

World Bank and UNICEF. 2009. *Abolishing School Fees in Africa: Lessons from Ethiopia, Ghana, Kenya, Malawi, and Mozambique*. Washington, DC: World Bank and UNICEF.

CHAPTER 2

The State of Textbook Provision in Sub-Saharan Africa

As already noted, data on textbook availability are patchy and often difficult to compare across countries. Even when textbooks are physically available in a school, they may not be available for students to use. Survey and anecdotal information suggest that available books might be locked up instead of distributed to students, either because they are costly and difficult to replace, teachers copy the text from them on a blackboard, or teachers are absent and students do not have access to the books.

The UNESCO Institute for Statistics (UIS) (2012) provides data on textbook availability for reading and mathematics in primary education for 22 Sub-Saharan African (SSA) countries. The data were collected through a special survey distributed to 45 SSA countries and cover the availability around 2010. The median availability was about 1.4 pupils per textbook for both reading and math. All but two of the countries had less than three students sharing one textbook for reading; for math, five countries had more than three students per textbook. It is not known to what extent the data reflect targets or actual availability. The difference can be important. A field survey for Uganda quoted in World Bank (2001, 11) found that actual textbook:pupil ratios were as low as 1:30 in some cases as compared to the official estimate of 1:7. The main reason for the discrepancy appeared to be a lower-than-expected book life caused by poor storage conditions and high losses and damages. Besides, student:textbook ratios are often quoted as prevailing at the time of supply of books and do not take into account subsequent distortions due to increases in enrollments. Also, surveys suggest that national averages vary considerably between different geographical areas as well as between pupils from different economic backgrounds. Book availability is typically lower further away from distribution centers. Table 2.1 illustrates this aspect.

Textbook availability is generally much lower for subjects other than reading and math. In Kenya in 2004—after the 2003 abolition of school fees and introduction of school capitation grants to support instructional materials including

Table 2.1 Variations in Book:Pupil Ratios in Primary Education

Country	Urban	Rural	Remote
Benin	1:10	1:10	1:10
Burundi	2:3	1:3	1:10
Côte d'Ivoire	1:1	1:1	—
Kenya	1:2	1:3	1:5
Namibia	5:1	1:10	1:15
Rwanda	1:3	1:3	1:3

Source: Read and Bontoux forthcoming.
Note: — = not available.

textbooks—average textbook:pupil ratios of 1:2, 1:3, and 1:3 were reached for English, math, and science subjects, respectively, compared to 1:4 for Kiswahili and 1:71 for geography, history, civics, and religious education (World Bank and UNICEF 2009, 141). Furthermore, partial data show considerable variation in availability by grade. UNESCO (1998) found that in 8 of 11 SSA countries covered, more than half the students in the highest grade had no math books. The Southern and Eastern Africa Consortium for Monitoring Education Quality found that more than half the grade 6 students in Kenya, Mozambique Tanzania, Uganda, and Zambia attended classrooms that did not have a single book (UNESCO 2008, 116).

For secondary education, a 2008 survey of 19 SSA countries found the following:

- All but one of the countries suffered from severe textbook shortages.
- Availability was best for language and math, but very poor in noncore subjects (eight students per book in the best case).
- Availability was much worse in rural areas; less than 5 percent of rural students had access to books in core subjects.

Common classroom practice was that the teacher had a textbook and copied its text on a blackboard (World Bank 2008).

While the paucity of data makes it difficult to know how the availability of textbooks has changed over the past two to three decades, textbooks were very scarce in SSA in the 1980s and 1990s. Across the region, the stagnation of education budgets in the 1980s and early 1990s led to declines in public expenditures per pupil, often resulting in the imposition of school fees and/or the need for parents to pay for textbooks. For example, data for 14 SSA countries for the late 1980s indicate that the majority of primary school students in most countries did not have textbooks or the number of students per book was very high (Lockheed and Verspoor 1990, 36). Books were particularly scarce in rural areas and mostly had to be purchased by parents, sometimes at subsidized prices. Colclough (1993) concludes,

> We have documented in this book the ways in which rural and urban schools... particularly in Africa... are often short on the most rudimentary items, including

exercise books, chalk, pencils, rulers, maps, and so on. But the most pressing need is for more textbooks.

World Bank (2002, 47) notes,

The desperate need for textbooks has been established in one appraisal report after another. Reported textbook:pupil ratios range anywhere from 1:5 to 1:10, or worse. Schoolchildren in tiny Sao Tome e Principe had no textbooks in the late 1980s. Across Zambia in 1993, schools had only one textbook in English for every five pupils, one in mathematics for every eight, and one in social science for every twenty. In the same year in Uganda, the ratio averaged 1:6 despite two previous infusions of textbooks under IDA credits. Acute shortages were most often caused by financial austerity, inadequate management, or logistic impediments. In Angola and Sierra Leone, books were destroyed in civil wars; in Burundi and Rwanda, in genocidal conflicts; and in Mozambique, in floods.

Finally, Colclough (2003, 183), providing data on book availability for nine countries (Ethiopia, Ghana, Guinea, Malawi, Mali, Senegal, Tanzania, Uganda, and Zambia) found that, on average, about five pupils shared one textbook, ranging from two in Ghana to ten in Guinea.

The much higher growth in domestic and external education funding since 2000 has eased some public budget constraints on textbook provision, including through the move away from school fees.[1] But this shift has also facilitated a strong (and welcomed) increase in enrollments and, thus, a sharp increase in the need for textbooks. For example, in 1990 the average gross enrollment ratio for SSA was only about 74 percent. The ratio was below 40 percent in about 10 countries, and the majority of the enrollment was in urban areas. By 2010 enrollment had increased dramatically, with the average gross enrollment ratio at 103 percent and only five countries with GERs under 80 percent. Over this 20-year period, primary school enrollment in the region more than doubled (from 62 million to about 133 million), including an increase of 46 million between 2000 and 2010. Secondary school enrollment nearly tripled over this period, from 15 million in 1990 to 44 million in 2010.

Both to cater to this rapid enrollment increase and to remedy the past low book provision necessitated a sharp increase in textbook provision over the past decade. But most SSA countries did not manage to respond adequately. The next chapter discusses some of the main reasons for countries' inability to respond.

Note

1. World Bank and UNICEF (2009) discusses fee abolition in Ethiopia, Ghana, Kenya, Malawi, and Mozambique.

References

Colclough, C., with K. Lewin. 1993. *Educating All the Children: Strategies for Primary Education in the South*. Oxford, UK: Clarendon.

Colclough, C., S. Al-Samarrai, P. Rose, and M. Tembon. 2003. *Achieving Schooling for All in Africa: Costs, Commitment and Gender.* Farnham, Surrey, U.K.: Ashgate Publishing.

Lockheed, M. E., and A. M. Verspoor. 1990. *Improving Primary Education in Developing Countries: A Review of Policy Options.* Washington, DC: World Bank.

Read, A., and V. Bontoux. Forthcoming. *Where Have All the Textbooks Gone? The Affordable and Sustainable Provision of Learning and Teaching Materials in Sub-Saharan Africa.* Washington, DC: World Bank.

UIS (UNESCO Institute for Statistics). 2012. "School and Teaching Resources in Sub-Saharan Africa." *UIS Information Bulletin*, UIS/IB/2012/9. Montreal, Canada: UIS.

UNESCO (United Nations Education, Scientific, and Cultural Organization). 1998. "Development of Education in Africa: A Statistical Review." Paper presented at the Seventh Conference of Ministers of Education of African Member States, UNESCO, Paris, April 24–28.

———. 2008. *EFA Global Monitoring Report 2009.* UNESCO, Paris.

World Bank. 2001. *A Chance to Learn: Knowledge and Finance for Education in Sub-Saharan Africa.* Africa Region Human Development Series. Washington, DC: World Bank.

———. 2002. "World Bank Support for Provision of Textbooks in Sub-Saharan Africa (1985–2000)." Africa Region Human Development Working Paper Series, World Bank, Washington, DC.

———. 2008. "Textbooks and School Library Provision in Secondary Education in Sub-Saharan Africa." Working Paper 126, Africa Region Human Development Working Paper Series, World Bank, Washington, DC.

World Bank and UNICEF. 2009. *Abolishing School Fees in Africa: Lessons from Ethiopia, Ghana, Kenya, Malawi, and Mozambique.* Washington, DC: World Bank and UNICEF.

CHAPTER 3

Factors Contributing to Textbook Scarcity

Drawing on a number of available country case studies, and based on reviews of the factors contributing to textbook scarcity in Sub-Saharan African (SSA) countries, there are many lessons drawn, of which four are of particular relevance:

1. **Large differences between countries.** While there are many constraints in every link of the textbook chain in most SSA countries, the severity of these constraints varies considerably depending on local context. Thus *no blueprint for removing the constraints to textbook provision that is applicable to all countries.* For example, to limit costs, some countries have streamlined curriculums to limit the number of textbooks required in each grade and have accompanied this with effective teacher guides. But most have not. Some countries have good local publishing and printing capability. Most do not. Some countries have found timely, effective ways of distributing textbooks to schools. Most have not. The cost and complexity of distribution varies enormously depending on country size, topography, and road networks. Finally, few countries have started to develop systems to ensure sustainable and predictable annual textbook financing.
2. **Neglect of system costs.** System costs are a crucial factor in explaining the high annual per-student cost of providing the number of textbooks required. For example, the median number of books needed in grade 6 in the nine countries surveyed in the Read and Bontoux (forthcoming) background study was 7, ranging from 4 to 10. The differences were even starker for secondary education: the median number was 10, but differences ranged from 6 to 15 (see tables 3.2, 3.3, and 3.4 in Read and Bontoux). To cut system costs, *countries need to streamline curriculums to limit both the length of books and the number required.* They also need to take into account the impact on textbook costs when deciding on curriculum revisions. Furthermore, although better paper and bindings increase unit costs, they extend book life—and so, in the long term, lower annualized costs, including distribution costs.

3. **Poor textbook planning, management, and monitoring.** *This is the most important constraint to resolving the high cost/low availability problem.* Most countries need to significantly strengthen their capacity to provide timely, reliable information on textbook availability and use, ensure low-cost procurement (by using price as a key factor in bid evaluations and reducing corruption), cut system costs, reduce book waste and damage—mainly by strengthening distribution and storage systems—and ensure predictable financing by establishing dedicated lines in their education budgets for teaching and learning materials (TLM).[1]
4. **Poor storage and distribution systems.** These cause high rates of book loss and damage and add significantly to the high textbook cost/low availability problem.

Because of this study's emphasis on the factors in each link of the textbook chain causing the high cost/low availability problem, it focuses on the cost and financing side of the problem by exploring two questions. First, what are the actual costs of meeting annual needs for textbooks, and what would these costs be in systems that achieve affordable unit and system costs? Second, what share of primary and secondary education budgets do SSA countries actually allocate to TLM, and what should these allocations be to ensure adequate provision of TLM to all students? These questions are addressed in chapters 5 and 6, respectively.

Note

1. Normally, this provision should be in the *recurrent* budget as textbooks are consumable item. However, the time between when a decision to purchase textbooks is made and the actual payment can be long. Thus, even when annual recurrent budgets provide for textbooks, anecdotal evidence suggests that ministries of education face problems in getting the money released from the ministry of finance before the end of the budget year.

Reference

Read, A., and V. Bontoux. Forthcoming. *Where Have All the Textbooks Gone? The Affordable and Sustainable Provision of Learning and Teaching Materials in Sub-Saharan Africa*. Washington, DC: World Bank.

CHAPTER 4

The Urgency of Addressing the Textbook Shortage in Sub-Saharan Africa

The urgency of improving the quality of education in Sub-Saharan Africa (SSA) has been stressed in many studies.[1] Similarly, numerous studies have also demonstrated the cost-effectiveness of investing in textbooks as a key element in any quality improvement strategy. A range of national and international assessments concur that high proportions of students in SSA complete education cycles without having acquired the requisite competences. In general, the remarkable increase in access since around 2000 has not been matched by comparable progress in learning outcomes. For example, the third Southern and Eastern Africa Consortium for Monitoring Educational Quality (SACMEQ) assessment, conducted in 14 countries in 2007, "highlighted acute deficits in learning achievements.... In Malawi and Zambia, over a third of grade 4 students had failed to acquire even the most basic literacy skills, implying that many were unable to read fluently after five to six years of primary education"[2] (see figure 4.1). Data from the Program on the Analysis of Education Systems, which covers Francophone countries, show similar results.

Improving education quality is likely to be the biggest challenge for SSA in achieving the Education for All goals. This is particularly so for low-income countries and for children from poor households, but is also a problem in middle-income countries. Low education quality causes students to disengage from learning and ultimately, drop out of school—reversing the gains from increased access. For students who persevere, low education quality leads to higher repetition rates and increased failure in acquiring requisite skills, competencies, and values. High dropout, repetition, and failure rates result in waste of resources that could have been better used to further expand access and improve quality. Failure to facilitate the acquisition of requisite competencies has negative impact on labor productivity (Hanushek and Woessmann 2008), on efforts to achieve inclusive growth, and on broader political, social, human, and cultural dimensions of development. Low education quality limits the opportunities for

Figure 4.1 Percentage of Grade 6 Students Reaching SACMEQ Skill Levels for Reading, 2007

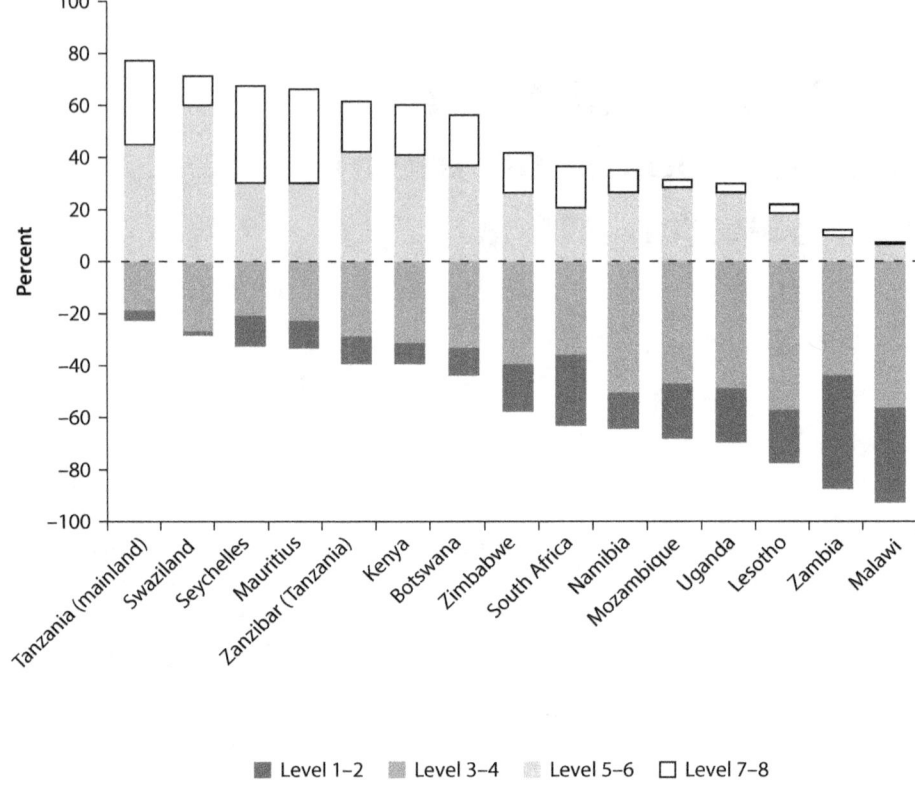

Source: Reproduced from UNESCO 2011, figure 1.37.

growth and the potential redistributive effects of education, thus reinforcing social and income inequalities and sustaining intergenerational poverty and marginalization.

As for the contribution of textbooks to addressing the quality challenge, there is widespread agreement that, apart from qualified and committed teachers, *no other input is likely to be more cost-effective than making high-quality learning materials available to all students.* This is especially the case in SSA, where many teachers have little training; classes are large; school years are short;[3] large percentage of parents are illiterate (the projected adult literacy rates for SSA for 2015 are 62 percent women and 76 percent for men); and households usually lack other reading materials. That is why countries known for their rapid education progress—such as the Republic of Korea, Singapore, and (more recently) Vietnam—gave high priority to universal access to high quality textbooks early in their drives for universal primary education (Fredriksen and Tan 2008).

A review of the evidence undertaken by Read and Bontoux (forthcoming) from the many studies conducted over the past several decades on the cost-effectiveness of textbooks and other learning materials in enhancing learning outcomes concluded the following:

- The evidence for the impact of textbook provision on student achievement in repeated research studies over the last 40 years is overwhelmingly positive. Even the few dissident studies accept that textbooks have a positive impact for good students in good schools.
- For textbooks to be effective they must be not only available but also regularly used in class and they must be in a language that is widely understood by students.
- Textbooks are the most cost-effective of all education inputs on student achievement because they provide significant impact at relatively modest cost; relatively small investments in textbooks and other learning and teaching materials have a disproportionately large impact on achievement compared to marginal investments in, for example, teachers.

Many of the early studies were conducted or sponsored by the World Bank as part of its efforts to enhance the quality of its increasing lending for education. For example, Heyneman and Farrell (1978) found a stronger, more consistent relationship between pupil achievement and the availability of books than between achievements and other school-related variables. Several other World Bank—sponsored studies in the 1980s also showed the important positive impact of textbooks on student learning (see for example, Jamison et al. 1981; Heyneman et al. 1984; Armitage 1986). Then as now, concerns about severe shortages of learning materials was driven by a general concern about the need to ensure that the increased access to education was associated with improved quality of learning. For example, Verspoor (1986) observed that

> Without quality improvement, many of the benefits associated with the tremendous growth of enrollments in developing countries may never come about. Research evidence and [World] Bank experience indicate the considerable potential contribution textbooks and other instructional materials can make to effective teaching and the improvement of the quality of education.

Similarly, the first World Bank (1988, 42) education sector policy paper for SSA notes,

> There is strong evidence that increasing the provision of instructional materials, especially textbooks, is the most cost-effective way of raising the quality of primary education. The scarcity of learning materials in the classroom is the most serious impediment to educational effectiveness in Africa. It is certainly here that the gap in education provision between this region and the rest of the world has grown widest.

By the early 1990s, improving the availability of high-quality textbooks was a top priority of both donors and African education ministers as reflected by the fact that the first biannual conference of the (then) Donors for Education in

Africa (later the Association for the Development of Education in Africa), in 1991, focused on textbooks. The conference proceedings concluded that textbooks in Africa fulfill three important purposes simultaneously:

1. They provide the main vehicle for the curriculum.
2. They are the main, if not the only, source of information for the teachers and students.
3. Examinations and student assessments are derived heavily from them.

In this situation, the textbook is effectively the curriculum (Read and Bontoux forthcoming).

More recent studies have confirmed the impacts found in the earlier studies. Based on SACMEQ data for 13 countries and Program on the Analysis of Education Systems data for 8 countries, Michaelowa and Wechtler (2006) found a change from no textbooks to a full coverage of one book per student increases student achievement by 5–20 percent of a standard deviation. Given that textbooks represent a much cheaper input than teachers and classrooms, the study concludes that textbooks constitute one of the most cost-effective education inputs.

There are a series of challenges associated with low textbook availability, which not only contribute to low textbook use and negatively impact learning achievement but also carry associated costs that are rarely measured.

Unless text books are delivered to schools, they are likely to languish at delivery points for lack of resources for transportation to schools. This adds to the requirement for, and maintenance of, either permanent warehousing facilities or temporary transit storage facilities. Increasingly, delivery costs are being built into textbook costs at the time of procurement and are difficult to disaggregate unless they are required to be stated separately during the procurement process. However, delivery points vary and some costs of delivery devolve to the schools or local governments. For example, in Ethiopia, books are delivered at the Woredas (equivalent to districts) and transportation to the school is the responsibility of the school and is to be paid for out of the school budgets. In Uganda, on the other hand, for recent textbook procurements, the delivery point has been the school.

In schools, textbooks need to be stored in a manner that ensures their safety as well as easy access by students, but not all schools have adequate storage space. Schools with smaller libraries pile books up, and schools that do not have libraries improvise by storing books in the head teacher's room, keeping them in makeshift storage rooms, or just dumping them wherever space is available. It is not unusual to see books lying in heaps on the floor. The best case scenario for use of text books is in schools that have proper space in libraries for storage, where students can borrow text books as per library rules in effect in the school, but actual use remains low since it is dependent entirely on the initiative of the students. There is no reported example of books being given to students on a rotational basis. Anecdotal evidence speaks to this state of affairs across SSA. Project reviews in some instances have taken cognizance of these challenges. In Uganda, where US$27 million (out of the total project cost of US$150 million) was allocated for provision of textbooks, the issue of utilization of textbooks is mentioned in almost all aide—memoirs of World Bank review missions since project inception. In Tanzania, World Bank missions visiting secondary schools in urban and rural areas in November 2009 and January–February 2010 observed that textbooks were conspicuously absent from classrooms and textbook availability in schools was very low. Despite this, when teachers were asked about their most urgent needs, textbooks were not mentioned as one of them (De Guzman 2010).

A study undertaken by the World Bank in Sierra Leone found that school administrators tend to hoard textbooks (Sabarwal, Evans, and Marshak 2012). The reasons cited were scarcity and lack of predictability of further textbook supply. School visits in Uganda also indicate that school managements take pride in showcasing the books where libraries exist but, in the absence of libraries, books appear to be treated as any other inventory item and are often dumped on the floor wherever space may be available with scant attention to the impact this might have on their condition. The Sierra Leone study cites "storing" of textbooks as a big reason for lack of student access to textbooks either in the class room or at home. It is no surprise, therefore, that the study found no impact of textbook provision on student learning outcomes.

When textbooks are scarce, their use by teachers remains low. If textbooks are scarce in schools, they are equally scarce in teacher-training institutions and teachers are not trained to use textbooks in the classrooms. Mohammad and Kumari (2007), in their study on the effective use of text books in Pakistan, report being informed that "for topics not taught in their training, the teachers fall back on traditional methods, namely rote memorization." In many African countries, where textbooks are not written to the curriculum, textbooks procured leave many curriculum topics uncovered and create further disincentive for teachers to use them. Incorporating textbooks into the teaching and learning process requires initiative on the part of the school management (head teachers) and teachers. High teacher absenteeism, overall low teacher engagement in the classroom, and lack of familiarity with textbooks and knowledge to effectively incorporate textbooks in teaching in the classroom, all contribute to poor textbook use.

Availability of libraries in schools and use of textbooks by both teachers and students are not given adequate attention either when designing programs that include textbook provision or in assessing the use or impact of textbooks provision on learning outcomes. The cost of nonuse of textbooks is not calculated; nor is the efficiency cost of low learning outcomes that are partly attributed to both low availability, as well as to the lack of use of available textbooks. If students are not being provided access to textbooks and teachers are not using them, the impact on student learning outcomes of textbook provision will be minimal or nonexistent. Instead of focusing on how to encourage use of textbooks, the failure of textbook provision to improve student learning outcomes is beginning to be used as an argument to challenge the role of textbooks in improving the quality of education.

Notes

1. Successive annual issues of the EFA Global Monitoring Report review the evidence available.
2. SACMEQ consists of 15 ministries of education in Southern and Eastern Africa.
3. The short effective school year is illustrated in surveys conducted in 2010 in Tanzania and Senegal (AERC and World Bank 2011), which found that the number of hours per day (average for all grades) during which primary school pupils were taught was 2 hours and 4 minutes in Tanzania against the official schedule of 5 hours and 12 minutes (i.e., 40 percent), and 3 hours and 15 minutes in Senegal as compared to the official schedule of 4 hours and 36 minutes (71 percent).

References

AERC (African Economic Research Consortium) and World Bank. 2011. "Service Delivery Indicators: Pilot in Education and Health Care in Africa." AERC and World Bank, Washington, DC.

Armitage, J. 1986. "School Quality and Achievement in Rural Brazil." World Bank Education and Training Department Discussion Paper EDT 25, World Bank, Washington, DC.

De Guzman. 2010. "Providing Textbooks for Secondary Schools in Tanzania: A Reconnaissance of Options." Working Paper, World Bank, Washington, DC.

Fredriksen, B., and J. P. Tan, eds. 2008. *An African Exploration of East Asian Education Experience*. Washington, DC: World Bank.

Hanushek, E. A., and L. Woessmann. 2008. "The Role of Education Quality in Economic Growth." Policy Research Working Paper 4122, World Bank, Washington, DC.

Heyneman, S., and J. Farrell. 1978. *Textbooks and Achievement: What We Know*. Washington, DC: World Bank.

Heyneman S., D. Jamison, and X. Montenegro. 1984. "Textbooks in the Philippines: Evaluation of the Pedagogical Impact of a Nationwide Investment." *Education Evaluation and Policy Analysis*, 6 (2): 139–50.

Jamison, D., B. Searle, K. Galda, and S. Heyneman. 1981. "Improving Elementary Mathematics Education in Nicaragua: An Experimental Study of the Impact of Textbooks and Radio on Achievements." *Journal of Educational Psychology* 73 (4): 556–67.

Michaelowa, K., and A. Wechtler. 2006. *The Cost-Effectiveness of Inputs in Primary Education: Insights from the Literature and Recent Student Surveys for Sub-Saharan Africa*. Paris: Association for the Development of Education in Africa (ADEA).

Mohammad, R., and R. Kumari. 2007. "Effective Use of Textbooks: A Neglected Aspect of Education in Pakistan." *Journal of Education for International Development* 3: 1.

Read, A., and V. Bontoux. Forthcoming. *Where Have All the Textbooks Gone? The Affordable and Sustainable Provision of Learning and Teaching Materials in Sub-Saharan Africa*. Washington, DC: World Bank.

Sabarwal, S., D. Evans, and A. Marshak. 2012. "Textbook Provision and Student Outcomes: The Devil in the Details." Manuscript. World Bank, Washington, DC.

UNESCO 2011 (United Nations Educational, Scientific, and Cultural Organization). *EFA Global Monitoring Report 2011.* UNESCO, Paris.

Verspoor, A. 1986. *Textbooks as Instruments for the Improvement in the Quality of Education.* Washington, DC: World Bank.

World Bank. 1988. *Education in Sub-Saharan Africa: Policies for Adjustment, Revitalization, and Expansion.* A World Bank Study. Washington, DC: World Bank.

CHAPTER 5

Factors Determining Textbook Costs

In discussing textbook costs, and the scope for reducing such costs, it is essential to distinguish between two types of unit costs: (a) unit textbook cost, i.e., cost of one single textbook, and (b) unit annual textbook cost, i.e., the annual cost of providing one student with the textbooks needed to deliver the curriculum in a specific grade. In addition to unit textbook cost, unit annual textbook cost depends on a number of system-related factors such as the number of books needed to cover the curriculum in a specific grade, the number of pupils who share one textbook (the textbook:pupil ratio), and average book life. Other system-related costs directly affect unit costs—for example, the number of topics covered in the curriculum determines the length of each textbook.

There are also factors that affect both *unit* and *annualized costs*. For example, higher quality paper and binding increase unit costs but decrease annualized costs by increasing book life. Decisions on textbook specifications (quality of paper, bindings, use of colors, etc.) become even more complex because there are factors that increase unit and/or annualized costs but also increase the impact of textbooks on learning. For example, using four colors instead of one, or higher quality illustrations, can increase both unit and annualized costs. But doing so might be cost-effective if the cost increase is lower than the increase in learning outcomes. Similarly, for the same unit cost, annualized costs can be lowered in ways that also lower the impact of books on learning outcomes—for example, if book life is increased by restricting textbook use in the classroom or by not allowing pupils to bring books home. The way the text is presented (in terms of font size, letter and word spacing, mix of text and illustrations, etc.) also has important implications for cost and effectiveness of textbooks (Abadzi 2006). This aspect is often neglected in textbook design.

Finally, for the same unit textbook cost and annualized cost of provision of teaching and learning materials (TLM), learning outcomes can improve through a judicious combination of textbooks and teacher guides. However, the cost factors also need to take into account the available resources and the need to provide universal access to textbooks. This further complicates the choices policy makers must make.

The fact that this report focuses on textbooks does *not* suggest that the availability of other TLM is not important. Materials such as teachers' guides, readers, school and classroom libraries, notebooks and other student supplies, maps and charts, and blackboards and chalk are essential to a meaningful learning experience. Textbooks are the focus here because in Sub-Saharan Africa (SSA) they are not only the most costly element of an effective TLM package but their production as well as effective use is also the most complex. In addition, the system improvements needed to address the high cost/low availability textbook problem will also help address the low availability of other TLM.

As emphasized in the Read and Bontoux (forthcoming) background report, comparisons of textbook costs need to be made with extreme care. Quoted *unit* book costs or prices are often not comparable because they include different cost elements, creating major distortions in the costs or prices quoted and making comparisons difficult. Sometimes the cost quoted is the *retail price*. Other times it refers only to the cost of *manufacturing* a textbook. And sometimes it is something in between, depending on the extent to which other cost elements such as manuscript development, publisher overhead, bookseller profit, and distribution costs are included (table 5.1). Similarly, the cost of reprinting an existing book differs from that of producing a new one. Further, commercially published textbooks often appear more expensive than those produced by state agencies because costs reported by state agencies often only include textbook development and manufacturing costs (printing and raw materials including paper),

Table 5.1 Two Examples of Retail Price Cost Components of Commercially Sold Textbooks in SSA (%)

Example 1		*Example 2*	
Textbook cost components[a]	Retail price (%)	Textbook cost components[b]	Retail price (%)
Royalties (costs of authorship)	7	Payment to authors	11
Origination (design, artwork, typesetting)	14		
Raw materials	12	Production costs (raw materials, prepress work, printing, and binding)	32
Manufacturing	10	Marketing costs (promotion and selling)	9
Publishers' overhead and profit (marketing, research, editing, administration, financing, bank charges and credit costs, premises, equipment, etc.)	28	Publishers' overhead and profit	16
Bookseller discount	25	Bookseller discount	23
Ocean freight	4	Distribution costs	9
Total	100	Total	100

a. Read and Bontoux (forthcoming), table 24 (a). See explanation in text.
b. World Bank 2002, table 2.3. Data based on a survey covering 21 publishers in 12 SSA countries.

while distribution and other costs are covered by other parts of the budgets of ministries of education.

And, for the same unit cost, annual student textbook cost varies widely depending on the targeted textbook:pupil ratios, length of book life, and number of books needed in each grade. These *system costs are* often more important than unit cost in determining *annual per-student costs* and can often be an obstacle to textbook availability and use. Finally, the generally high rate of textbook loss and damage during storage and distribution is another key determinant of the total costs of reaching the goal for textbook provision.

The chapter 5 sections "Unit Textbook Costs" and "Annualized per-Student Textbook Costs" summarize key factors affecting unit and annualized book costs while "Actual Unit and Annualized Textbook Costs in SSA" provides examples of cost differences between countries and grades in primary and secondary education. The section "Interventions and Scope for Reducing Textbook Costs" summarizes key interventions and scope for cost reduction.

Unit Textbook Costs

The reasons for differences in unit textbook costs between SSA countries can be classified into seven categories: (a) origination, (b) raw materials, (c) manufacturing, (d) procurement methods, (e) publisher overhead and profit, (f) bookseller discounts, and (g) distribution and storage. Table 5.1 illustrates the relative contribution to *retail textbook price* of the key cost elements in commercially produced textbooks. Though the cost components do not correspond neatly to each link in the textbook chain, or to the seven categories, they illustrate the relative importance of key links in that chain. The left-hand part of the table refers to an actual costing of a 96-page primary textbook printed in four colors with durable production specifications, intended for *retail sale* in SSA in 2011 by a leading African textbook publisher. The right-hand side refers to the cost structure of an average African textbook in the mid-1990s, based on a survey of 21 publishers in 12 SSA countries. While the cost components in the two examples are not directly comparable, the main components are still illustrative of the cost composition of the retail price. In particular:

- Author royalties accounts for 7–11 percent of retail price in the two examples.
- Prepress work, raw materials (including paper), printing, manufacturing, and binding costs account for about a third of the retail price in both cases (36 percent in the example for 2011 and 32 percent in the one for the mid-1990s). The 2011 example breaks this further down into 14 percent for origination, 12 percent for raw materials, and 10 percent for printing and binding.
- Publisher overhead and profits contribute more to the retail price than raw materials and manufacturing together, accounting for 28 percent in the first case and 25 percent in the second if marketing costs are added to publisher overhead and profits.

- Bookseller discounts also account for about a quarter of the retail price in both examples, again contributing more to retail price than paper and manufacturing. This cost element applies only if books are supplied through the retail trade. If a ministry of education supplies books, their distribution costs are lower for the publisher and higher for the ministry.

Thus *publishers and booksellers* account for about half the retail price of textbooks—and might offer the largest scope for lowering costs.

As a corollary, the cost components that often get the most attention in discussions of textbook cost in SSA—prepress costs, manufacturing, and raw materials—do not represent *the main cost component of the retail price*. World Bank (2002, 18) notes that "on average, the retail price of commercially published textbooks was three times the cost of manufacture." Similarly, the Read and Bontoux study (forthcoming, 11) concludes, "On a 'rule of thumb' basis the manufacturing cost is usually considered to represent between 15–20 percent of the retail price of a textbook.... Raw materials may comprise 30–60 percent of the cost of manufacturing (depending on production specifications and sources of supply), but they do not comprise the same percentage of the retail price."

Table 5.2 provides a similar cost breakdown for *state publishing*. Here costs such as publisher overhead may not be included; most of these are subsumed elsewhere in the government budgets. Since table 5.2 does not include all costs cost components, these percentages are not comparable to those of table 5.1.

The rest of this section discusses the seven unit textbook cost components. The sequence of the discussion largely follows the links in the textbook chain, but again, the cost components do not correspond neatly to these links.

Origination

Origination costs involve developing a textbook manuscript and readying it for printing. The classification adapted for this report also includes payments to authors. In addition, the costs include developing the textbook concept; identifying and commissioning authors to write the manuscript; reviewing, testing, and editing the manuscript; deciding on and commissioning illustrations; verifying the proofs; and identifying, selecting, contracting, and supervising manufacturing. Clearly, the origination costs depend on whether the manuscript is developed from scratch or it is an adaptation or reprint of an existing text.

Table 5.2 Textbook Price Components for State Publishers

Component	Percent
Origination costs (typesetting, design, artwork, etc.)	20
Raw materials	40
Manufacturing	35
Royalties/authorship	5

Source: Read and Bontoux forthcoming, table 24b.

The organization of these activities varies. A main distinction is between whether they are carried out by commercial publishers, by state publishers, or by the ministries of education. Read and Bontoux (forthcoming) review the evolution of textbook publishing in SSA (see box 5.1). Prior to independence, most textbooks were either imported unchanged from commercial publishers in the respective European countries or, in some cases, developed or adapted by local branches of those publishers. After independence, state monopolies in textbook publishing grew quickly as part of countries' efforts to take control of their education systems, including by introducing new subjects and content that reflected national and African history, culture, and aspirations. In turn, this required textbooks that would reflect these new programs. In Francophone countries, the publishing function was normally carried out by national pedagogic institutes that were strengthened (often through external funding) to develop textbook manuscripts and ready them partly or fully for printing.

Since the 1990s, there has been a reversal to relying more on the private sector, often through public-private partnerships, not only for printing, but also for originating text.[1] These private partners often also write textbooks while the state establishes the system and rules of provision; evaluates submitted textbooks against agreed criteria including degree of relevance to and coverage of curriculum, creates approved textbook lists, determines textbook selection, and monitors and supervises system performance. African publishers have

---

Box 5.1 Evolution of Textbook Publishing in Sub-Saharan Africa

- The state textbook publishing experiment of the 1960s, 1970s, and 1980s did not resolve textbook provision problems and from the 1990s onward state publishing structures have been widely demolished and replaced by private sector publishing involvement.
- Low state textbook prices were achieved by only including printing and raw materials costs and ignoring the costs of staffing, accommodation, operation, plant, and even authorship, which were paid by governments often as part of the education budget.
- Countries are increasingly adopting textbook provision systems based on approved lists of competing textbooks from which schools can select and pay through school grants.
- The provision of market access to private sector textbook publishers has led to a rapid growth in local publishers and local publishing capacity throughout SSA.
- Multinational publishers are now much less dominant in anglophone SSA but more so in francophone countries. Authorship capacity is available in most countries for most subjects and, when needed, experienced international or regional authorship can be combined with local authorship teams to build skills and experience.
- Locally published lower secondary textbooks are significantly cheaper than imported textbooks originally published for developed world markets and thus carrying developed world overheads.

Source: Read and Bontoux forthcoming.

experienced rapid growth both domestically and regionally. Local authorship is now widespread for primary and some junior secondary textbooks especially in the Anglophone countries. At the senior secondary level, many countries continue to import titles written for other markets. But that too is expected to change, aside from more neutral subjects, such as math and science, because using international authors and publishers allows for larger print runs. Also, as discussed in chapter 8, the role of e-books and other electronic materials may be larger for such subjects.

Table 5.3 provides details of the sources of authorship, publishing, manufacturing, and raw materials in the countries surveyed for this study. Local authorship, publishing, and manufacturing now is quite widespread for primary and lower secondary education, while raw materials are still sourced dominantly from overseas although often via local or regional middlemen.

Ownership of textbook copyright can be a contentious issue (Read and Bontoux forthcoming; World Bank 2002, 13–14; World Bank 2008, 59–61). A textbook is intellectual property and is subject to national legislation and international copyright agreements. This implies that the right to publish a book has value and affects its price, especially the price of reprinting it. As suggested by table 5.3, many SSA countries prepare the manuscripts themselves, especially for primary education; they sometimes contract out other publishing functions, such as editing, design, illustration, and printing, and often also delivery to schools. In such cases, it is important to clearly distinguish between the government as *publisher* and a private sector company contracted to *supply publishing services* to the government. Often, for a variety of reasons, a government might decide to share publishing rights with a commercial publisher. In all cases, it is important to use specialists to draw up contracts between ministries of education and publishers to avoid problems that can hinder timely provision of textbooks and increase costs.

Finally, the use of local languages or mother tongue for instruction is an important consideration for TLM. This is not the place to discuss the merits of such choices; suffice it to say that there is a broad consensus that students perform better and learn faster if they start their education in a familiar language. In this report, the main interest is the *cost implications* of providing TLM in local languages. This choice affects origination costs as well as printing costs per book in countries that cannot realize economies of scale due to short print runs. It might also affect distribution costs in cases where separate distribution systems are required. But, even if *unit* textbook cost might be higher if several local languages are used, *this factor should not be decisive* as to whether or not to use mother tongue instruction.

- Origination costs account for a relatively small part of textbook retail price (see table 5.1), though such costs depend on how well developed a particular language is. Many local languages are widely spoken, often in several countries, have an established orthography and literature, and are used by newspapers, television shows, and radio stations. For such languages, extra development

Table 5.3 Sources of Authorship, Publishing, Manufacturing, and Raw Materials for Grades 1, 6, 8, and 11

Country	Authorship/publishing			Manufacturing			Raw materials		
	Local	Regional	International	Local	Regional	International	Local	Regional	International
Benin	All grades	Secondary	Secondary	All grades	Secondary	Secondary			All grades
Burundi	All grades		All grades			All grades			All grades
Chad	Secondary		All grades			All grades			All grades
Côte d'Ivoire	All grades		All grades	Primary		All grades			All grades
Kenya	All grades		Secondary	All grades					All grades
Madagascar	Primary and junior secondary	Upper primary and secondary	Secondary	All grades		All grades			All grades
Mali	All grades			All grades					All grades
Namibia	All grades	Upper primary and secondary			Upper primary and secondary			All grades	All grades
Nigeria	All grades		Upper secondary	Some primary		Primary/secondary			All grades
Rwanda	Primary and junior secondary	All grades	All grades		All grades	All grades			All grades

Source: Read and Bontoux forthcoming.

costs of TLM are unlikely to be the factor determining whether to use such languages as means of instruction. Nor should costs resulting from low print runs. As discussed below, for most books printed in black and white, economies of scale can be achieved at print runs as low as 7,500–10,000 copies. At the other extreme are many "small" languages, often spoken in areas where there are other more widely spoken languages, and that may not have an established orthography, literature, or authorship capacity.
- Any additional costs would need to be weighed against the learning benefits that research has shown result from use of the mother tongue in the early years of basic education.

The choice of language of instruction is not straightforward, especially in countries with multiple languages. In addition to pedagogical implications, such choices often have wide-ranging cultural and political ramifications, possibly even determining the long-term survival of many "small" languages. From a purely pedagogical point of view, harnessing the positive impact on learning outcomes that come from teaching in local languages requires other inputs—especially teachers who are trained to teach in the local languages *as well as* in the main language that will be used beyond the first few grades of the primary cycle. The severe shortage of such teachers is often the main constraint on successfully making the transition from mother tongue to main language instruction. Therefore, in countries with several languages, the role that these languages should play as means of instruction, and the resulting need for textbooks in such languages, must be decided as part of a country's language policy. Unfortunately, many countries do not yet have clear policies on language of instruction or have not thought through the challenges of implementing such policies.

Raw Materials
Textbook production specifications—in terms of quality of materials—such as paper and binding—are crucial in determining both *unit* and *annual* per-student textbook costs. In general, better quality paper, cover, and bindings means higher unit costs as does the number of colors used. But better quality paper, cover, and binding also extends book life, lowering annual costs of replacement. Many other specification details are important to costs, such as the size of the printed page to get the most economic use of paper. This is particularly important in SSA where paper typically represents 45–70 percent of total manufacturing costs as compared to about 30 percent in industrialized countries (World Bank 2002, 15). The price of paper is volatile, and major printing houses have an advantage over small firms. In addition, some SSA countries impose import duties on paper and printing equipment. Such duties make local printers more costly than external printers when imported textbooks are duty free.[2]

Table 5.4 illustrates the relationship between production specifications, length of book life, and unit cost. The example refers to actual prices quoted in September 2011 from a leading textbook printer in Mumbai, India, and shows

Table 5.4 Comparative Prices for One- and Four-Year Textbook Specifications

Item	Title	Size	Cover pages	Text pages	Cover colors	Text colors	Text paper	Cover card	Binding style	Print run	US$ price FOB
1	Primary TB	7.44 x 9.68"	4	96	4	4	62 gsm	180 gsm	Saddle stitch	75,000	0.464
2	Primary TB	7.44 x 9.68"	4	96	4	4	80 gsm	250 gsm	Saddle stitch	75,000	0.553
3	Primary TB	7.44 x 9.68"	4	96	1	1	62 gsm	180 gsm	Saddle stitch	75,000	0.381
4	Primary TB	7.44 x 9.68"	4	96	1	1	80 gsm	250 gsm	Saddle stitch	75,000	0.540
5	Secondary TB	7.44 x 9.68"	4	144	4	4	62 gsm	180 gsm	Perfect bound	20,000	0.788
6	Secondary TB	7.44 x 9.68"	4	144	4	4	80 gsm	250 gsm	Section sewn	20,000	0.969
7	Secondary TB	7.44 x 9.68"	4	144	1	2	62 gsm	180 gsm	Perfect bound	20,000	0.624
8	Secondary TB	7.44 x 9.68"	4	144	1	2	80 gsm	250 gsm	Section sewn	20,000	0.780

Source: Reed and Bontoux forthcoming.
Note: FOB = free on board; gsm = grams per square meter.

how quality of paper, cover card, and binding style for a one-year and a four-year textbook life, respectively, affect unit costs. Compared to the four-year, the one-year book life specifications opt for lower quality text paper and cover card and cheap, nondurable bindings. Otherwise, the print runs, formats, and use of color are identical between both. The four-year and the one-year specifications are typical to the kind of specifications that a publisher would require a printer to achieve the required book life.

For primary education, the differences in *unit cost* between the one-year and four-year specifications for print runs range from 19 percent to 50 percent. For secondary education, the differences are 23 percent and 26 percent. But the *annual per-student cost* for a one-year textbook would be as much as 2.7 times higher than for a four-year textbook if the *unit* price is 50 percent higher and 3.4 times in case the unit price is 19 percent higher. This does not account for the fact that longer book life does not mean that all books will last the whole period and that some of the older books may need to be placed. It might also have other implications, such as whether students can take books home. But even taking such factors into account, the potential savings offered by a longer textbook life will be substantial and are an important element in deciding on how to make adequate textbook provision more affordable.

In addition to affecting textbook life and costs, many design factors—such as the number and complexity of designs and illustrations, the use of colors, the readability of the typeface, and the quality of the paper—affect the effectiveness of textbooks as learning tools. For color, there has been a lot of discussion whether multicolor textbooks are worth the additional costs. In most countries, primary school textbooks are now printed in full color and secondary textbooks in one or more colors. In full-color books, acceptable economies of scale and prices can be reached at between 30,000–50,000 copies. Black and white books can achieve the same from print runs for as low as 7,500–10,000 copies. Thus full-color books can become very expensive for small countries where print runs are small.

Thus, textbook specification and design are important factors in determining unit and annual student costs as well as the effectiveness of the book as a learning tool. Bad choices can add substantially to unit and, especially, annual costs by shortening book life, as well as reducing the pedagogical effectiveness of the book.

Manufacturing

Once a textbook manuscript has been developed and its specifications decided, where to print the books—nationally, regionally, or internationally—is a major part of the publishing process in SSA and has generated considerable debate. The World Bank (2002, 15) noted, "Few book publishers today own their own printing plants. The expense of modern presses has led to concentration in the industry, and publishers often arrange printing in cities and countries other than their own." Textbooks are by far the important market for national publishers and printers in most SSA countries. Thus, the ability to develop a vibrant national printing (and possibly publishing) industry depends on the extent to which textbooks are printed locally. This has often required making tradeoffs between the desire to manufacture textbooks locally and the desire to avoid having the education system, parents, and pupils pay the price for doing so through more costly and/or lower quality textbooks.

The evolution of textbook printing in Africa, the choice between private and public publishing, and the pros and cons of using national, regional, and international national printing are summarized in box 5.1. Of late, national and regional commercial African publishers have become more competitive. But book printing is specialized work, requiring printing and bookbinding equipment and skills beyond those required for newspapers, magazines, and other commercial products. Also, to be able to reap economies of scale, publishers normally follow an integrated *teamwork* approach, in which the full range of required skills are applied from conceptualization through planning, writing, development, and production to the finished book, rather than a *linear approach*, handling each task in sequence. The latter approach—commonly used by smaller publishers such as those operated by ministries of education—is less efficient. It means printing one book at a time in one or a limited number of printers, and requires greater investment in prepress and book storage until all the books are ready for distribution. The advantage of sourcing printing through larger regional and international printers is the possibility of using several printers simultaneously, which greatly reduces printing lead time and thus avoids tying up equipment and storage space over a long period. International textbook printers frequently work three shifts per day and amortize plant costs effectively as a result. They also invest in high efficiency plants producing at lower costs. Many national printers, on the other hand, work one or two shifts often on less efficient reconditioned older plants with higher levels of downtime and wastage.

The length of print runs is a key factor in determining unit printing costs. The length of print runs needed for the costs to plateau is quite sensitive to the number of colors used. Figure 5.1 illustrates that for a full-color book, the cost

Figure 5.1 Long Print Run Cost-Benefit Curve

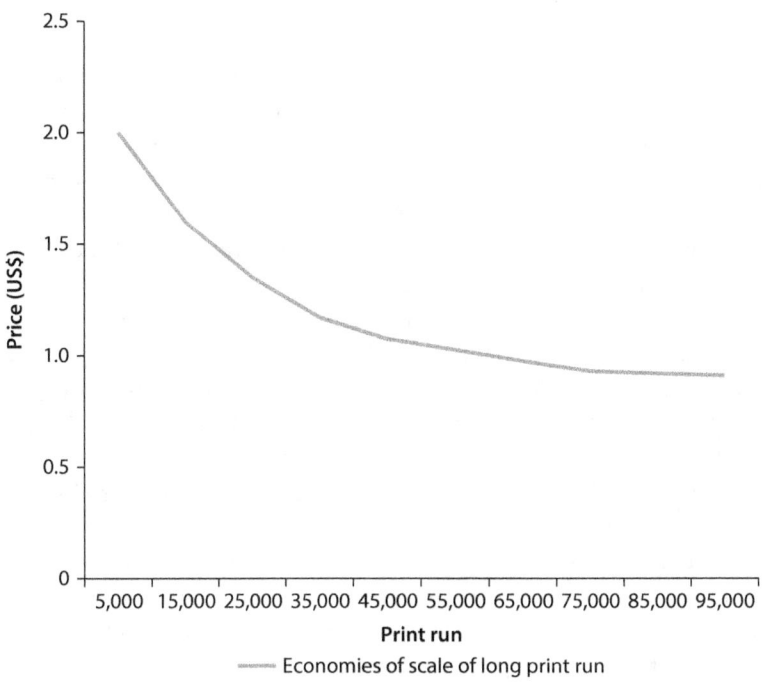

savings decline quite sharply after 35,000–50,000 copies. For black-and-white books, the cost plateau is often reached after 7,500–10,000 copies. Thus, modern printing technology makes it possible to achieve significant economies of scale at relatively low print run levels.

The extent to which economics of scale can be achieved in local printing depends on the number of books needed—which depends on the number of pupils enrolled in the grade the book is intended to serve. For any given enrollment figure, the number of books required also depends on a number of system-related factors, such as the textbook:pupil ratio, the length of textbook life, and the number of languages used. And for any given value of these factors, longer print runs can be obtained by, for example, printing more books for storage and later distribution and by publishing books in languages that are used in more than one country. But as discussed below, poor storage and distribution capacity makes this impractical in many SSA countries.

Procurement Methods

This section does not discuss the pros and cons of different methods of textbook procurement. It is limited to emphasizing that, in the past, poor governance and ineffective procurement have caused high textbook costs in SSA and other regions. The problem is being addressed in various ways, often resulting in substantial price reductions. As discussed below, ensuring effective and competitive procurement is perhaps the most important action needed to address cost factors related to publisher and bookseller costs (see chapter 5, "Unit Textbook Costs"). For example:

1. A growing number of countries are breaking government monopolies and turning to the private sector for textbook publishing and distribution. Bontoux (2002, cited in DfID 2010) notes that in 2002 when Uganda chose a private publisher through a well-designed competitive process, textbook prices fell by two-thirds and textbook durability and presentation quality increased substantially. In the early 1990s, Brazil was able to reduce textbook prices by 30–40 percent using a similar approach.
2. In many SSA countries, the move toward the private sector and competitive bidding has been associated with a shift toward decentralized textbook supply systems based on ministry of education–approved textbook lists and school-based choices financed through grants to individual schools or school districts. In many countries, this has been an integral part of school fee abolition policies (e.g., Ghana, Kenya, Tanzania and Mozambique; see World Bank and UNICEF 2009).
3. Using textbook price and production specifications as key factors in textbook evaluation and contracting is an effective way of reducing price and enhancing quality. In evaluating the bids, a good balance has to be struck between the weights given to textbook price and qualitative aspects. Read and Bontoux (forthcoming) suggest that giving price 25–30 percent of evaluation points usually provides the right balance. The study also notes that good examples of bid documentation and evaluation methodology, instruments, and criteria for different types of procurement are readily available. World Bank (2008, 11) notes that giving prominence to price in evaluation and approval process has helped countries such as Ghana, Kenya, Tanzania, and Togo reduce the prices for secondary education textbooks.
4. Finally, effective and transparent textbook procurement requires good professional supervision. In some cases, cooperation with civil society organizations can help limit corruption, improve the timeliness of delivery, and, more generally, help hold governments more accountable for poor delivery of public education services. The comparator paper study for the Philippines (see chapter 7) provides an excellent example of how cooperation between a ministry of education and civil society organizations helped enhance transparency and limit corruption in textbook procurement and delivery through sustained civil society participation in the monitoring of textbook procurement, warehousing, and delivery processes.

In sum, the effectiveness and transparency of textbook procurement have likely improved over the past decade. The problem is part of the wider concern on the need for greater accountability for public sector service delivery. And, as the Philippines example shows, enhancing such accountability may need collective action involving cooperation between different actors through both top-down (from ministries of education) and bottom-up (from users and

Publishers' Overhead, Profit, and Marketing

As noted, publishers' overhead, profit, and marketing are the most important factor for high retail textbook prices in SSA. The overhead includes salary and other costs related to editorial, administration, storage, rent, utilities, financing, and so on. Even though this cost component and bookseller discounts account for about half of the retail price, they receive less attention in considerations about factors causing high textbook cost than costs related to manufacturing and raw materials. As an illustration, the cost-reduction strategies summarized by Read and Bontoux (forthcoming). focus on actions to reduce system cost, waste, and distribution. The authors make no direct mention of the cost-reduction strategy proposed to the scope for reducing publishers' overhead and bookseller discount. But other sections of the same study note several actions that can help.

- Promoting competitive procurement (as discussed in chapter 5, "Procurement Methods") can help.
- Switching from developed to developing country local publishing would tend to reduce the profit and overhead component of the price because these cost elements are higher for publishers in developed countries. This potential saving would need to be weighed against potential savings resulting from sourcing printing from larger regional and international printers discussed in chapter 5's section "Manufacturing."
- Speeding up payments to publishers would reduce the publishers' bank borrowings and thus reduce the financing costs. The Read and Bontoux (forthcoming) study notes that there are many examples of governments delaying payment by two years or more. The costs of financing this cash flow gap have to be built into the quoted prices.

One reason why publishers' overhead and profit have received less attention in the past is likely to be that state monopolies and/or the ministry of education played a dominant role in publishing textbooks.

Booksellers' Discount

As noted, bookseller discounts account for about a quarter of textbook retail price in SSA. This includes a profit margin for booksellers as well as distribution costs. If textbooks are supplied in bulk to a government, this discount is subtracted from the retail price. The normal trade distribution discount in SSA countries is 25 percent. In cases where the contract requires direct distribution to schools by publishers, the distribution cost is often between 10–15 percent. If the supply is only to districts rather than to schools, the distribution charge may be 6–7 percent. And where supply is only to a central warehouse in the capital city, the charges are often only 5 percent even when supplied from international printing sources.

Textbook price markups by book sellers can be a problem in decentralized financing systems where publishers sell through local booksellers or traders. Publishers expect that booksellers should be able to cover the costs of supply and make a profit out of the discount they make. However, Read and Bontoux (forthcoming, 100) note the following:

> Publishers have reported cases in many SSA countries where booksellers have marked up the official retail price by 20–50% in order to increase their profitability. Sometimes the mark-up may be agreed with a head teacher and the agreed mark-up is then shared. Once again, it is difficult to quantify the extent of pricing mark-ups but they may be very extensive, particularly in rural and remote areas where most schools will not be able to access competitive sources of supply. Schools often have no access to official price lists or even to the recommended price lists of individual publishers. Booksellers sometimes produce their own price lists which are given to schools. If there is a lack of…supervision of commercially supplied approved textbooks then price mark-ups are more likely. Price mark-ups… undermine the effectiveness and sustainability of textbook provision systems… [and] increase rural/urban inequity in the system.

In short, especially in countries relying on decentralized procurement, this cost factor is important in determining book price as well as the effectiveness of book distribution to schools.

Distribution and Storage

Many SSA countries face serious problems in ensuring secure storage and reliable distribution of textbooks to schools. In addition to affecting learning outcomes through lower and often late textbook delivery, *poor warehousing and distribution systems raise the costs of ensuring the desired level of textbook availability*. About half of the textbooks are wasted in some countries, and 20 percent annual loss and damage is not unusual. Apart from the obvious impact on overall costs of textbook loss during the storage and distribution processes, damage to the books that are delivered shortens textbook life and thus increases system costs, the frequency of distribution, and distribution costs. DfID (2010, 7) notes that

> [B]ecause state book distribution systems were underfunded and were not paid on evidence of completed delivery, there was no motivation to perform efficiently. Books would be stuck in district or sub-district warehouses with no attempt to deliver them to schools, because there was no district transport and no funds to rent transport. Many of the district stores were in such poor condition that books suffered serious damage from rain, damp, dust and vermin. In Guinea it was reported that over 60% of textbook stocks were "lost" during transportation. In 2004, the national audit office in Ghana reported that 50% of districts inspected had no records of book supplies to schools.

Based on the many country case studies, the following can be concluded:

- Many textbook distribution systems in SSA are seriously dysfunctional, leading to very high levels of stock loss and damage, resulting in substandard textbook:pupil ratios in a majority of SSA countries.
- Most governments and development partners are unaware of the extent of wastage caused by poor national distribution systems. Thus, there are relatively few examples of sustained, well-planned, professional project components aimed at upgrading book distribution capacity and performance.
- Textbook distribution is still maintained as a state or ministry of education activity in many countries, but the ministries rarely have the finances, facilities, knowledge, and skills needed to perform this job. This is particularly true at the critical district levels where storage and delivery from districts to schools represent very common problems in most SSA countries.
- Commercial book trade involvement is constrained in most countries because of the lack of creditworthy wholesale and retail outlets in rural and remote areas.
- Effective planning is constrained by inaccurate data and by lack of simple, professional management and monitoring systems designed to ensure that schools receive and maintain the supplies that they require. Creation of such systems—including a reliable, computerized database trained staff, and effective system supervision and accountability mechanisms—would improve the situation dramatically in most countries.

Thus, the damage and waste caused by poor warehousing and distribution systems is an important contributor to the high textbook cost/low availability problem. In the past, donors have supported system improvements. But those are only part of the problem. Alternatives to state management need to be considered through greater use of public-private partnerships. These partnerships would do the following:

- Use the existing wholesale and retail book trade if it has the necessary capacity, national coverage, finance, and professionalism
- Ask publishers to include distribution costs to schools in their tendered prices and pass the distribution burden to publishers
- Tender school-level distribution to professional haulage companies.

All three approaches are partially used in some countries. Read and Bontoux (forthcoming) cite Rwanda as an example where in 2011:

> [P]ublisher distribution had achieved deliveries to 96% of all schools including districts with difficult to access schools requiring head portage through rugged mountainous areas. The motivation for this performance was that the publishers could not be paid until they had demonstrated successful delivery. This contrasts with years of ineffective distribution organized by the Ministry of Education.

But for this to work, ministries of education must have the right information to give to subcontractors and must have management and monitoring systems in place to make sure that the subcontractors have performed satisfactorily. One of the most powerful incentives for good performance is the incentive of payment only on confirmed delivery.

Annualized per-Student Textbook Costs

As noted, for any given level of *unit* textbook cost, *annual per-student textbook cost* depends on *system costs* related to the number of textbooks needed to deliver the curriculum in any given grade, the textbook:pupil ratio, and textbook life. The impact of these three factors on annual per-student costs can be expressed as the following:

$$\text{Annual per-student textbook costs} = \frac{\text{Unit cost} \times \text{number of textbooks per grade} \times \text{textbook:pupil ratio}}{\text{Average textbook life}}$$

Obviously, the concept of annual per-student costs is a more useful indicator of affordability and sustainability than simple unit book cost. The impacts of these three factors are discussed below.

Curriculum Impact on Textbook Needs

Based on a review of many SSA countries, Read and Bontoux (forthcoming) as well as DfID (2010) noted that curriculum is often designed (and revised) with little consideration to TLM cost implications and that this neglect causes high annual per-student textbook cost. The curriculum has an impact on this cost in several ways:

1. The number of subjects covered by the curriculum determines the number of textbooks needed in each grade. The number of subjects has tended to increase over the past several decades. In the nine countries surveyed for the study, the number of books needed ranged from 2 to 9 in grade 1 (the median was 4), from 4 to 10 in grade 6 (median 7), from 5 to 15 in grade 8 (median 8), and from 7 to 16 in grade 11 (median 8). Similarly, World Bank (2008) found that among 19 SSA countries studied, the number of textbooks needed ranged from 6 to 14 titles for lower secondary education.
2. The curriculum also affects the length of each textbook. Because of the relatively short length of the actual school year in most SSA countries and the tendency to add subjects in which teachers are not trained, many syllabuses are overloaded. As a result, textbooks often provide far more content than what can be covered during the school year, making them longer and more costly than necessary.
3. There are several country-specific examples of the lack of consideration of textbook costs when revising curriculums, both when it comes to extending the number of subjects covered and making existing textbooks obsolete.

4. When decisions are made on the TLM needed to deliver the curriculum for any given grade, it should be decided what should be covered in textbooks and what can be covered in teacher guides (supplied at one book per class rather than at one book per student) or in library books (supplied in small numbers per school rather than per class).

In short, countries can make textbook provision more affordable by paying more attention to the TLM costs associated with different curriculum choices. It would be better to have fewer books covering the essential parts of the curriculum—and to ensure that all students have access to these books—than to have a proliferation of subjects, leading to a larger number of books required but not made available.

Textbook:Pupil Ratios

As covered in previous sections, data on textbook availability in SSA are scarce and unreliable. But what interests us here is the impact of the textbook:pupil ratio on annualized per-student book costs. That relationship is clear: other things equal, moving from a 1:1 to a 1:2 ratio halves the annualized per-student costs. However, it is less clear what impact this has on the learning process. For example:

- Most governments and educationalists want every student to have access to textbooks in key subjects at a 1:1 ratio. When this is not possible, the impact of the textbook:pupil ratio on learning is unlikely to be linear. For example, a study for the Philippines showed that the decline in the impact was relatively small when moving from a ratio of 1:1 to 1:2, but more substantial when moving from 1:2 to 1:3 (World Bank 2002).
- The number of subjects covered, and thus the number of books needed, is normally lower for grades 1 and 2 than for grades 5 and 6. There is also scope for varying book:student ratios depending on the subject as well as combining lower textbook:pupil ratios in some subjects with more/better teacher guides and other materials.
- Regardless of grade, having a 1:1 ratio may be more important for some subjects (e.g., reading and math) than for others (e.g., geography or social studies). Many studies suggest that the highest priority should be given to reading.

In short, countries need to carefully consider textbook:pupil ratios by grade and subject as well as the mix of different types of TLM to maximize the learning impact of their TLM budgets.

Textbook Life

As noted, textbook life depends on the quality of paper, binding, and cover as well as of storage and distribution, among other factors (such as whether students can take books home). For example, going from a one-year to a four-year book life, at an extra cost of 25 percent, would lower annualized per-student textbook costs to one-quarter of that of a one-year life.

But other factors would need to be taken into account. For costs, a four-year book life could add textbook storage and maintenance costs. On the other hand, to provide new books only every fourth year could significantly reduce storage wastage as well as distribution and administrative costs. There are well-documented examples that a textbook life of four to five years is achievable with the right specifications, quality manufacturing, good distribution systems, and good care and conservation in the classroom (see DfID 2010; Read and Bontoux forthcoming).

Actual Unit and Annualized Textbook Costs in SSA

The lack of comparability of unit textbook costs across countries has already been noted. This point is well illustrated by the unit costs for grades 1, 6, 8, and 11 for nine SSA countries. Table 5.5 summarizes the data for grade 1. The unit cost ranges from US$0.75 to US$7.00 with a median of US$3.00. There are also large differences in system costs. The number of books needed ranges from two to nine with a median of four. An assumed book life ranges from one to four years with a median of two to three years. Eight of the nine countries aimed at a 1:1 textbook:pupil ratio.

The corresponding data for the other three grades showed similar, wide country differences:

- **Grade 6**. Unit cost ranged from US$0.75 to US$7.50 (median US$3.00), required number of books from 5 to 10 (median 4), and target book life from one to five years (median 3.5). Of the nine countries, seven aimed for a textbook:pupil ratio of 1:1, the actual ratio ranging from 1:1 to 1:3. The median annual cost per student was US$5.38, ranging from US$3.00 to US$14.00.

Table 5.5 Unit, System, and Annualized per-Student Costs for Grade 1, Selected Countries

Country	Price (US$)	Number of books	Assumed book life (years)	Target textbook:pupil ratio	Annualized costs per pupil (US$)
Benin	2.70	6	n.a.	1:1	n.a.
Burundi	1.00	9	2–3	1:1	3.00–4.50
Chad	5.00	2	1	1:1	10.00
Côte d'Ivoire	3.00	3	1	1:1	9.00
Kenya	3.80	8	4	1:1	7.65
Madagascar	0.75	8	2	1:1	3.00
Mali	4.50	3	2–3	1:1	4.53
Namibia	7.50	3	5	1:2	2.25
Rwanda	2.50	4	4	1:1	2.25
Median	**3.00**	**4**	**2–3**	**1:1**	**4.14**

Source: Read and Bontoux forthcoming.

- **Grade 8.** Unit cost ranged from US$1.00 to US$15.00 (median US$6.00), required number of books from 5 to 15 (median 8), and target book life from one to five years (median four). Four of the seven countries providing data aimed for one book per pupil, but the textbook:pupil ratio ranged from 1:1 to 1:3. The median annualized cost per pupil was US$10.00.
- **Grade 11.** Unit cost ranged from US$1.00 to US$15.00 (median US$11.50), required number of books from 7 to 16 (median 8), and target book life from four to five years (median five). Four of the seven countries providing data aimed for one book per pupil, but the textbook:pupil ratios ranged from 1:1 to 1:5. The median annualized cost per pupil was US$11.00, ranging from US$3.00 to US$24.00.

It is illustrative to look at the key factors explaining the large difference in unit cost between the two countries that had the lowest (Burundi) and the highest unit costs (Namibia) in all four grades (Read and Bontoux forthcoming).

- The low unit cost for Burundi (US$1.00 in all four grades) is largely explained by the fact that the cost includes only raw materials and printing.[3] As suggested by table 5.1, these costs normally account for less than one-third of the retail price. In addition, several factors contribute to low printing costs: The books are small, are printed in only two colors, and have fewer than 100 pages. Further, Burundi is one of the few SSA countries with a single national language of instruction, and there are no competing textbooks. Both factors facilitate long print runs. The books are reprints of older books, and are printed internationally. Finally, Burundi is a small country, which helps lower distribution costs—though these are not included in the cost quoted.
- The high unit cost in Namibia (US$7.50 in grades 1 and 6; US$15:00 in grades 8 and 11) represents the opposite case. The country has competing textbooks despite its small market, which is further fractionalized by providing instruction in up to 7 of the 17 local languages. The textbooks have high standards including full-color production. This makes it difficult to benefit from economies of scale given the relatively small population. Also, price is not a factor in the evaluation process. Finally, Namibia is a vast country with high distribution costs, which is included in the price.

This illustrates the difficulties in comparing book prices between countries without a great deal of local knowledge about which cost elements are covered. It also shows again that manufacturing costs (printing and raw materials) comprise only an (often minor) part of retail book price. However, in determining its textbook policies, a government needs to take a holistic view, because other costs (related to, e.g., authorship, editorial, financing, distribution, overheads) generally have to be covered somewhere in the government's budget.

Finally, table 5.5 illustrates the impact of *system factors* on annualized per-student costs: While Namibia has, by far, the highest unit cost, the country still has the lowest annualized per-pupil cost. This is explained by the fact that only

Table 5.6 Average Unit Price, Number of Books, and Cost of Textbook Set for Grade 9, 2007, Selected Countries

Country	Price (US$)	Number of books	Cost of textbook set (US$)
Botswana	11.07	9	99.60
Cameroon	8.95	13	116.30
Côte d'Ivoire	7.64	8	61.10
Ghana	5.19	8	41.60
Kenya	3.80	15	57.00
Lesotho	18.75	8	150.00
Malawi	7.06	12	84.70
Nigeria	4.61	7	32.69
Tanzania	4.25	6	25.30
Togo	9.92	6	59.50
Uganda	15.00	10	155.19
Median	**7.64**	**8**	**61.10**

Sources: Read, Bontoux, and Buchan (2007); DfID (2010); most data are also in World Bank (2008).

three books are required in grade 1, two pupils share a book, and a book life of five years is higher than in other countries.

Table 5.6 shows average unit textbook cost, required number of books, and average cost of a textbook set for grade 9 in 11 SSA countries. As already illustrated by the data shown above for grades 8 and 11 for nine countries, this demonstrates further that for secondary education, also, there are wide differences between countries in unit and system costs. Average unit cost ranges from US$3.80 to US$18.75 (median US$7.64), number of books required in grade 9 from 6 to 15 (median 8), and average cost of a textbook set from US$25.30 to US$155.19 (median US$61.10).

Interventions and Scope for Reducing Textbook Costs

Priority Interventions

Decisions on cost and financing issues related to adequate and affordable TLM provision must be made within a comprehensive process involving many players and policy issues inside and outside the education system. The process starts with the student needs, as defined by the curriculum; continues through the development, publishing, procurement, financing, and distribution of the textbook; and ends with the students' use of the textbook, inside and outside of the classroom. Throughout this process, numerous factors in each link of the textbook chain affect textbook quality, availability, and cost as well as the annual financing needed. And decisions in one link of the chain affect others. So, to prepare, implement, and monitor interventions to successfully address the low availability/high cost textbook problem faced by most SSA countries requires the following:

1. **Adequate institutional capacity** in each key link of the textbook chain
2. **Political will** to ensure adequate availability of textbooks for all students.

On the first point, the most important recommendation of this report is to establish the sustainable and transparent systems needed to do the following:

- **Select cost-effective TLM** by taking into account TLM costs when developing and/or revising the curriculum and making choices about different types of TLM.
- **Develop and implement cost-reduction strategies** by reviewing the full range of possibilities for reducing the total annual costs of providing all students with the required TLM. This means giving much more attention to three cost elements that largely determine total annual TLM cost and financing needs: system costs, publishers' overhead and bestsellers' discounts, and rates of textbook loss and damage during storage and distribution.
- **Monitor each school's textbook availability and need** for annual replenishment to replace used books and cater to enrollment increase. Such monitoring also permits holding school managers more accountable for the textbooks received.
- **Ensure predictable and sustainable financing** to allow for timely procurement and delivery of the books needed.

System improvements need to be accompanied by political will to address the factors preventing pupils from having affordable textbooks.[4] This is needed to build the systems required, implement cost-reduction policies, and mobilize sustainable financing. (The last element is discussed in chapter 6). While inadequate financing is causing textbook shortage, this constraint should not be binding if governments build sustainable systems and address the factors causing the low availability/high cost problem.

Scope for Reduction in Textbook Costs

So what is the scope for reducing textbook costs if countries successfully implement cost-reduction policies in unit costs, system costs, and distribution costs? For unit costs, Read and Bontoux (forthcoming) conclude as follows:

> Although it is a complex task to compare textbook costs in different countries there should be no reason why primary and secondary textbooks should not be made available at reasonable costs if the system design is well-performed and if print runs are large enough to achieve reasonable cost benefits. On this basis, primary textbook unit costs of US$2–3 and secondary textbook costs of US$4–6 should normally be achievable, but these figures cannot necessarily be achieved in every case.

This scope for cost reduction is repeated in other reports such as World Bank (2008, 13) and DfID (2010, 23).[5] It is well below costs for most of the countries for which retail prices (rather than manufacturing costs) are shown in tables 5.5 and 5.6, especially for secondary education. For example, if Burundi and Madagascar are excluded for primary education (since their unit costs do not reflect retail price), the median price for the other seven countries in table 5.5 is US$4.20 and only two countries have a price in the US$2–3 range. Among the

11 countries in table 5.6, four had average prices in the US$4–6 price range for grade 9, against a median price of US$7.64.

For system costs, almost all of the nine countries surveyed for this study aim at a textbook:pupil ratio of 1:1 in primary education. In reality, this ratio is seldom reached. So, other things being equal, progress toward this target will increase system costs. But there is considerable scope, in most countries, for decreasing system costs by increasing textbook life and, especially, by reducing the number of books required in each grade on a 1:1 basis, but increasing the number of teachers guides and library books. For example, in Rwanda (in 2008) the annualized per-student textbook costs for grade 1 were lowered by 59 percent (from US$5.23 to US$2.15) by reducing the number of textbooks from six to three (supplied at a textbook:pupil ratio of 1:1). The reduction in textbooks was supplemented with increased supply of teachers' guides for all subjects and books for classroom libraries.

More textbooks are also needed in higher grades and, especially in secondary education. But given the severe book shortage, it makes sense to use the same approach here as well—that is, provide textbooks on a 1:1 basis in a limited number of core subjects and then provide teachers guides and more extension materials in school libraries to stimulate student-centered learning. Furthermore, as discussed in chapter 8, various electronic TLM are starting to play a key role in secondary education in many countries.

For distribution costs, reducing costs related to distribution, damage, and loss might be the cost component where increased attention in an overall cost reduction strategy could have the greatest payoff.

As noted, data available on unit textbook cost are seldom comparable between countries, and the factors causing the high cost/low availability textbook problem faced by most SSA countries vary considerably. Therefore, strategies for cost reduction must be country-specific; there is no blueprint that fits all countries. But most countries have considerable scope for savings on both unit and, especially, system costs and thus on the overall costs of providing all students with the books needed to meet national targets.

Notes

This chapter draws heavily on Read and Bontoux (forthcoming).

1. Over a 30-year period, many countries outside Africa have also gone full circle in textbook publishing. For example, Singapore started by using commercially produced books mostly ill-suited for Singapore. It then moved to textbooks developed by education ministry agencies to be consistent with education reforms, be low-cost, and complement the shortage of well-trained teachers, but printed by private printers. In 1996, Singapore shifted back to commercially produced textbooks, reflecting syllabuses approved by the Ministry of Education (Ang 2008).
2. Duty free import is covered by the 1950 Florence Agreement on the Importation of Educational, Scientific and Cultural Materials to which many SSA countries are signatories, and the 1982 Nairobi Protocol to that agreement.

3. Madagascar had the lowest unit cost for grades 1 and 6 (US$0.75). As for Burundi, these costs clearly do not include all cost components. Data for Madagascar were not available for grades 8 and 11.
4. This is different from many East Asian countries where provision of high quality, low-cost training material was given high priority early on in drive to universalize primary education. Later on, governments gave high priority to ensuring that textbooks were updated. For example, the most important task of Vietnam's third education reform completed in 1996 was the replacement of textbooks in all schools (Fredriksen and Tan 2008, 27–29).
5. The authors of the Read and Bontoux (forthcoming) study have authored or contributed to many of these reports.

References

Abadzi, H. 2006. *Efficient Learning for the Poor: Insights from the Frontier of Cognitive Neuroscience*. Washington, DC: World Bank.

Ang, W. H. 2008. "Singapore's Textbook Experience 1965–97: Meeting the Needs of Curriculum Change." In *Toward a Better Future: Education and Training for Economic Development in Singapore since 1965*, edited by L. S. Kong, G. C. Boon, B. Fredriksen, and J. P. Tan, 69–95. Washington, DC: World Bank.

Bontoux, V. 2002. "Comparison of Textbook and Teachers' Guide Prices and Physical Specifications between Cycle 6 (1998) and Cycle 8 (2002)." IBD for Department for International Development, London.

DfID (Department for International Development). 2010. "Learning and Teaching Materials: Policies and Practice for Provision." Practice paper, DfID, London.

Fredriksen, B., and J. P. Tan, eds. 2008. *An African Exploration of East Asian Education Experience*. Washington, DC: World Bank.

Read, A., and V. Bontoux. Forthcoming. *Where Have All the Textbooks Gone? The Affordable and Sustainable Provision of Learning and Teaching Materials in Sub-Saharan Africa*. Washington, DC: World Bank.

Read, A., V. Bontoux, and A. Buchan. 2007. "Secondary Textbook and School Library Provision in Sub-Saharan Africa: A Review Based on 19 National Case Studies." World Bank, Washington, DC.

World Bank. 2002. "World Bank Support for Provision of Textbooks in Sub-Saharan Africa (1985–2000)." Africa Region Human Development Working Paper Series, World Bank, Washington, DC.

———. 2008. "Textbooks and School Library Provision in Secondary Education in Sub-Saharan Africa." Working Paper 126, Africa Region Human Development Working Paper Series, World Bank, Washington, DC.

World Bank and UNICEF. 2009. *Abolishing School Fees in Africa: Lessons from Ethiopia, Ghana, Kenya, Malawi, and Mozambique*. Washington, DC: World Bank and UNICEF.

CHAPTER 6

Textbook Financing

Chapter 5 summarized key textbook cost issues and provided information on *actual* unit and annualized per-student textbook costs in Sub-Saharan Africa (SSA). It also highlighted key cost elements in the textbook chain and reviewed scope for reducing these costs. This chapter follows the same approach in discussing textbook financing. It first highlights some key issues in textbook financing ("Issues"), and then provides some data on actual financing by the three main sources of financing in SSA: governments, parents, and donors ("Sources and Methods of Textbook Funding in SSA" and "Government Textbook Financing in SSA"). Based on actual information on public education financing for primary and secondary education for about 30 SSA countries, "Estimated Share of the Primary Education Budget Needed for the Adequate Supply of Textbooks" and "Estimated Share of Secondary Education Budget Needed for Adequate Supply of Books" then explore what share of these budgets would need to be allocated to textbooks in, respectively, primary and secondary education for different levels of annualized textbook costs per student. Finally, "Impact of External Aid" highlights the impact of foreign aid.

Issues

The shortage of comparable data that bedevils the analysis of textbook availability and costs is even more prevalent for textbook financing. This raises a number of issues in analyzing how much of SSA countries' education budget is spent on textbooks. First, as discussed in the section "Impact of External Aid," in preceding decades, donors have played a major role in funding textbooks. However, it is difficult to quantify this role. Based on data for 27 SSA countries, UNESCO (2012, 146) estimates the *median* share of aid in *total government and donor spending* on education for the period 2004–10 at about 22 percent. Given donors' extensive support for textbooks over decades, and the poor progress in establishing sustainable and predictable national funding, it is likely that aid accounts for much more than 22 percent of the median country's *textbook* budget. In many countries, external aid has been the *only* nonparental textbook funding.

Second, an analysis of the *share* of education budgets used on textbooks is complicated by the fact that it is not clear to what extent external funding (for textbooks as well as for other purposes) is included in the public education expenditure data reported by countries. Given the importance of aid in many countries, different approaches in this regard would considerably affect conclusions regarding the share of *total* public education budgets (government plus donor financed) that is used for textbooks.

Third, shortage of *adequate* and *predictable* financing is a key constraint on the availability of textbooks. Both elements are important: The *level of financing* must be sufficient to allow adequate provision of teaching and learning materials (TLM) to all pupils. But to prepare, produce, procure, and distribute textbooks is a time-consuming process. Therefore, the financing must be *predictable* to enable publishers, government agencies involved in textbook provision, and school managers to ensure that the textbooks needed are available in the classroom at the start of the school year. Moreover, unreliable funding and payment also affect textbook prices. Read and Bontoux (forthcoming) provide data on the level of adequacy, regularity, and predictability of various types of TLM in the nine countries surveyed for this study. For textbooks and readers, three of the nine countries reported funding to be "adequate" and "regular." Of the eight countries providing data on "predictability," three reported funding to be predictable. The adequacy, regularity, and predictability of funding for TLM other than textbooks were much worse in all countries.

Four, while shortage of financing often is thought to be *the* key cause of low textbook availability in SSA, as discussed in chapter 3, shortage of textbooks is caused by a combination of factors of which financing is only one. And, to the extent financing is a binding constraint, it is partly because of the failure to address the factors causing high prices that make unaffordable the volume of financing needed. The responsibility for this failure must be shared between the countries and their development partners. For example, most donor-supported national education plans include the costs of providing textbooks. But few if any plans include systematic textbook cost reduction strategies of the type suggested in chapter 5's section "Interventions and Scope for Reducing Textbook Costs."

The rest of this chapter explores how much of public education budgets SSA countries spend on textbooks, and how this compares with what they would need to spend to ensure adequate textbook provision if successful cost-reduction strategies were implemented.

Sources and Methods of Textbook Funding in SSA

The three main sources of textbook funding in SSA are governments, parents, and external sources. Their relative importance varies widely between countries, over time, and by level of education. Table 6.1 illustrates the situation in grades 1, 6, 8, and 11 for the nine countries surveyed for this study. In brief, governments fund (through different approaches including through external aid)

Table 6.1 Sources of Textbook Funding

Country	Grade 1	Grade 6	Grade 8	Grade 11
Benin	S	S	P	P
Burundi	S	S	S	S
Chad	F	F	P	P
Côte d'Ivoire	F	F	P	P
Kenya	C	C	C P	C P
Madagascar	F	F	P	P
Mali	F	F	F	F
Namibia	F	F	F	F
Rwanda	C	C	C	C

Source: Reed and Bontoux forthcoming.
Note: C = purchased by schools with government funding; F = free government supply to schools; P = parent purchase; S = government provides limited free safety net supplies.

the textbooks provided in grades 1 and 6 while parents pay for secondary school textbooks in five of the nine countries.

Parents play a major role in textbook funding, although this role has changed over time. After independence, many SSA countries aimed to provide free education, in particular at the primary level, including free textbooks. For example, Ghana abolished primary school fees in 1961, and Kenya and Tanzania did so in 1974. These policies were largely reversed during the economic decline of the 1980s and 1990s but were reinstated during the past decade following improved economic conditions and increased donor support. In many cases, textbooks were financed through school grants (Fredriksen 2009).

Despite improvements in public funding over the past decade, parents still play a major role in funding textbooks even at the primary level. For example, in the Democratic Republic of Congo parents, and to some extent donors, have funded whatever few textbooks have been available. The share of parent financing is even higher in secondary education. World Bank (2008) found that of 18 SSA countries surveyed, whatever textbooks were available in secondary education were entirely financed by parents in 11 countries, by governments (including through external aid) in 5 countries, and by a mix of government and parents in 2 countries. This represents a severe strain on household budgets and on parents' ability to send their children to school, especially for poor people.

It is sometimes argued that parents should contribute to the funding of textbooks. In addition to supplementing resources, the argument goes, this would have other benefits such as encouraging pupils to take better care of their books, stimulating the industry through increased demand, because each child would have a book (though it may also stimulate a second-hand market). When textbooks are the property of the school and must be left at the school, pupils cannot use them after school or during school vacations. In households where there is no other written material, the environment can be very detrimental to learning. Hallak (1990, 203) notes that "even poor families are usually willing to pay if a textbook costs less than 1% of per capita gross domestic product (GDP), but the most acceptable range is 0.1–0.5%." In 2008, the average GDP for SSA excluding South Africa was about US$800. At 0.5 percent, that would be US$4 per book. However, as discussed in chapter 5, the actual cost is much higher since a student requires several books in each grade. Also, the average number of children per family is much higher in SSA than in other regions.

Developing countries in other regions are also given as illustrations that parents can pay for textbooks. For example, in Vietnam, an estimated 60–70 percent of pupils buy their own textbooks, the government limiting its free supply to the 30–40 percent of children living in particularly poor and remote areas. However, as with so many country comparisons of book cost and affordability, these situations are not comparable. First, book prices in Vietnam are very low, ranging from the equivalent of one-third to two-thirds of a U.S. dollar (see Fredriksen and Tan 2008, 29). This is a far cry from the prices in most SSA countries. Second, as noted above, family size in SSA is much larger than in East Asia. Thus, the cost to a family of paying for textbooks in Vietnam is a fraction of what it is in most SSA countries.

Finally, donor funding of textbooks is important in most SSA countries both because of the high volume and because of the lack of predictability. As regards the latter, often one or more donors have provided major support to replenish the stock of textbooks or to prepare and procure new textbooks to reflect new curriculum. There may be years without support, then—because the stock has not been maintained—the same or other donors may repeat the process. This type of off and on involvement reflects a third aspect of donor funding: Despite much support for capacity building in the textbook sector, this support has generally failed to help countries put in place a *sustainable system* for annual textbooks provision.[1]

Government Textbook Funding in SSA

There is a broad consensus on the case for public funding of textbooks in low-income SSA countries, especially in primary education. This argument is based on quality as well as education equity reasons, given the cost-effectiveness of textbooks as a pedagogical instrument as well the high level of poverty and the documented difficulty of poor families to pay for textbooks. However, as discussed in chapter 2, despite the paucity of comparable data, it is clear from the many country case studies available that the *actual* provision of all types of TLMs falls far short of any reasonable minimum standard.

This section discusses public funding of textbooks from three angles: It first highlights various *targets* set for such funding over the past 25 years, then presents some data on *actual* funding and, finally, explores what *share of primary and secondary education budgets would need to be spent on textbooks* to meet national targets for free textbook provision.

Budget Targets for Textbook Funding

Over the years, targets have been proposed for the share of education budgets that should to be allocated for textbooks in order to ensure adequate supply. For example:

- World Bank (1988, 46) assessed that an annual expenditure of about US$5 per pupil should meet minimum requirements for primary education.[2] The paper estimated the unit recurrent public expenditures per primary school pupil at US$48 in 1983.[3] This would imply a spending on TLM corresponding to about 10 percent of recurrent primary education expenditures. This is broadly of the same magnitude as the current *actual* level of funding. (See chapter 6's section "Actual Share of Government Budgets Allocated to Textbooks.") However, this estimate must be interpreted in the context of the 1980s where most SSA countries faced (a) stagnating education budgets, leading to declining unit cost per pupil, and (b) textbook prices largely set by the world market at a time when the values of most national currencies were declining. This *desired* level of spending of 10 percent of the primary education budget on TLM was far above the *actual* share at that time which was less than 1 percent (Colclough 1993, 168; World Bank 1988, 141).

- The (former) Organization of African Unity advised in the mid-1990s that member states allocate "a minimum of 25 percent of their budgets and 6 percent of gross domestic product to education, that a minimum of 50 percent of education budgets be allocated to primary education, and that the proportion of education budgets allocated to learning materials should be increased to 14 percent" (World Bank 2002, 22).

- Colclough et al. (2003) studied the education budgets in nine countries including the provision of textbooks (Ethiopia, Ghana, Guinea, Malawi, Mali, Senegal, Tanzania, Uganda, and Zambia). The study concludes that "the availability of learning materials is usually grossly inadequate. In most countries, textbooks were provided by international agencies whose expenditure was generally included in the capital budget. Expenditure on learning materials by the governments was mainly limited to office supplies, teaching aids, exercise books, and pens and pencils. Classroom observations in the countries showed that these supplies were frequently insufficient and sometimes not available at all" (111). The study estimates that to provide adequate level of funding for TLM, the allocation would need increase by a factor of 4 (median increase for the nine countries).[4]

- The "Indicative Framework" developed by the Fast Track Initiative (FTI, now GPE) established targets for the share of the primary education budget needed for *nonsalary* recurrent expenditures. In 1999–2000, the 33 SSA countries for which data were available spent on average 24 percent of their recurrent education budget on nonsalary expenditures.[5] The target was to reach 33 percent by 2015 to cover all types of nonsalary recurrent inputs, but no specific target was set for TLM.[6] Rasera (2003) estimates that (at constant prices) the 33 percent would represent about US$23 per pupil in 2015 and that a "minimum level of nonsalary inputs" at the school level would correspond to US$16, of which TLM could account for US$6.43 (40 percent). Of this, textbooks would account for US$1.70, which would correspond to 2.5 percent of the primary education budget. The remainder (US$4.73 per pupil) would be for other materials such as UNICEF's Essential Learning Package that includes essential teaching and learning materials such as notebooks, pencils, pens, and so on, as well as one dictionary per classroom, a library of 40 books per classroom, and teacher guides for seven subjects, and collective classroom materials. Together, this would amount to 9.3 percent of the budget. The study also estimates the costs of a "desirable level of inputs" at US$33 of which textbooks alone would be US$5 (ADEA 2005, 298–301).[7]

- In 2003, Burkina Faso became the first country to implement UNICEF's Essential Learning Package (UNICEF 2008). More countries have followed, including Benin, Chad, the Democratic Republic of Congo, The Gambia, Guinea, Mali, Mauritania, Niger, Nigeria, Senegal, and Sierra Leone.

- Finally, many governments fund TLM through school grants. For example, when Kenya established its free primary education policy in 2003, the Ministry of Education established a capitation grant equivalent to US$14 per pupil per year. The expenses financed by the grant were split with 35 percent for textbooks (with the aim of achieving over time a textbook:pupil ratio of 1:3 in lower primary grades and 1:2 in higher grades), 28 percent for other TLM, and 37 percent for other recurrent costs at the school level (World Bank and UNICEF 2009, 133).

Actual Share of Government Budgets Allocated to Textbooks
Table 6.2 shows data on the share of primary and secondary education budgets spent on TLM. Again, there are large differences between countries. However, it is difficult to know the extent to which this reflects differences in *actual* spending or simply different levels of completeness of the data. The median share for the 15 countries covered for primary education is 6.6 percent, ranging from 0.7 percent in Togo to 15.0 percent in Guinea, and 5.0 percent for secondary education, ranging from 0.4 percent in Cameroon to 14.8 percent in Niger. Only 3 of the 11 countries reporting data for both levels of education spent a higher share on secondary than on primary education. It could reflect both that parents play a larger role in funding textbooks for secondary than for primary education and that textbooks are even scarcer in secondary education.

As already noted, compared to the 1980s and 1990s, financing for public education in SSA has increased considerably over the past decade, from around

Table 6.2 Share of Total Recurrent Public Education Budgets for Primary and Secondary Education Spent on TLM, 2009 or Most Recent Year (%)

Country	Primary education	Secondary education
Burundi	5.5	—
Burkina Faso	4.8	0.7
Cameroon	7.1	0.4
Chad	14.8	9.1
Comoros	10.3	—
Guinea	15.0	5.3
Lesotho	3.0	—
Madagascar	1.2	0.9
Malawi	11.3	6.9
Mali	10.2	12.8
Niger	6.6	14.8
Rwanda	10.8	5.0
South Africa	2.9	2.9
Togo	0.7	1.0
Uganda	1.7	—
Median	**6.6**	**5.0**

Source: UNESCO and UIS 2011, 83.
Note: — = not available.

2 percent annually to about 9 percent. However, the data available make it difficult to assess to what extent this increase has affected public funding for TLM. The UNESCO Institute for Statistics noted,

> There are many inadequacies in the reporting of international comparable variables related to education quality.... Ministries of education rarely have good data on the quantities or costs of textbooks and other teaching materials. (UNESCO and UIS 2011, 83)

This is partly explained by the fact that some governments (as illustrated above for Kenya) fund nonsalary recurrent expenditures including textbooks through block grants directly to districts or schools. As already noted, it is not known to what extent donor funding of TLM is included in the public recurrent education expenditures reported by governments. Most such funding is likely not included, because textbooks are provided directly under donor-funded projects or, as noted by Colclough et al. (2003, 111), are included in the capital budget.

In view of the data limitations, it is difficult to assess the trends in budgetary allocations to TLM. This said, the share of the primary education budget allocated to such material was only about 1 percent around 1983 (median for 17 countries; World Bank 1988), 2.6 percent around 1993 (median for 20 countries; UNESCO 1998), but 6.6 percent around 2009. This may suggest an improvement over time.

Estimated Share of Primary Education Budget Needed for Adequate Supply of Textbooks

Budget Share Needed

This section explores the share of the budget for primary education that would be required to provide textbooks for all students according to different levels of unit and system textbook costs. Table 6.3 attempts to answer this question using *actual* enrollment and budgets in primary education for the 30 SSA countries for which such data were available. The expenditure data refers to *total recurrent and capital expenditures*. Ideally, the calculations should be based on the recurrent budget only. However, since the recurrent budget is high at 91 percent of the total budget in the median country, using the recurrent budget would only increase modestly the budget shares presented below. Also, as noted earlier, some countries (and donors) include their support for textbooks in the capital budget.

The budget shares shown in table 6.4, columns 5–8 are derived by multiplying the annualized per pupil textbook costs under different assumptions for unit and system cost with the actual number of students (column 2) and then expressing the result as a percentage of the actual budget in column 4. The share of the education budget shown in columns 5–8 are based on the following unit and system cost assumptions:

1. **Column 5.** Unit textbook cost: US$2:00. System costs: (a) five books needed per grade, (b) 1:1 textbook:pupil ratio, and (c) one-year book life. The unit cost represents the lower end of the US$2–3 price range for textbooks for primary education suggested possible in Read and Bontoux (2015), also referred to as the R&B study. System costs (a) and (b) correspond roughly to the median *targeted* values for primary education for the nine survey countries in Read and Bontoux (forthcoming). The one-year textbook life is a more ambitious replacement target than that found in most countries. These unit and system costs yield an *annual per pupil textbook cost* of US$10.00.
2. **Column 6.** The shares are based on the same assumptions as those in column 5 apart from that textbook life is increased from one to three years. This yields an *annual per pupil textbook cost of* US$3.30.
3. **Column 7.** Same assumptions as for column 6 apart from the fact that the number of textbooks needed per grade is reduced from five to three. This yields an *annual per pupil textbook cost* US$2.00.
4. **Columns 8.** Shows the budget shares required if unit and system costs equal the medians for grade 1 and 6 for the nine countries surveyed in Read and Bontoux (forthcoming). For these two grades, the median unit cost was about US$3.50, the median number of books required in each grade was five,[8] the median textbook:pupil ratio was 1:1, and the median book life was three years. This resulted in an annualized per pupil textbook cost of US$5.80.

The last line of table 6.3 provides the median budget shares required for the 31 countries for four different combinations of unit and system costs.

Table 6.3 Estimated Share of Primary Education Budget (Recurrent and Capital) Needed to Provide Textbooks for Different Unit and System Costs

Country (1)	Year (2)	Enrollment (000s) (3)	Budget (000s) (4)	Required budget share (%)*			
				(a) (5)	(b) (6)	(c) (7)	(d) (8)
Benin	2009	1,719	172,195	10.0	3.4	2.0	5.8
Botswana	2009	331	179,286	1.8	0.6	0.4	1.0
Burkina	2010	2,048	213,437	9.6	3.2	1.9	5.6
Burundi	2010	1,850	67,617	27.4	9.1	5.5	15.9
Central African Republic	2010	637	12,742	50.0	16.7	10.0	29.0
Cameroon	2010	3,510	267,370	13.1	4.4	2.6	6.7
Cabo Verde	2009	71	40,062	1.8	0.6	0.4	1.0
Chad	2010	1,727	109,035	15.8	5.3	3.2	9.1
Comoros	2008	111	24,896	4.5	1.5	0.9	3.6
Congo, Rep	2010	705	231,553	3.0	1.0	0.6	2.4
Congo, Dem. Rep.	2010	10,572	109,634	91.7	30.6	18.3	73.4
Ethiopia	2010	13,635	793,073	17.2	5.7	3.4	2.6
Gambia, The	2010	229	26,266	8.7	2.9	1.7	5.1
Ghana	2010	3,860	550,242	7.0	2.3	1.4	4.1
Guinea	2008	1,364	37,587	36.3	12.1	7.3	21.0
Kenya	2006	6,076	749,007	8.1	2.7	1.6	4.7
Lesotho	2008	396	63,661	6.2	2.1	1.2	3.6
Madagascar	2009	4,324	142,094	30.4	10.1	6.1	17.6
Mali	2009	1,926	173,478	11.1	3.7	2.2	6.5
Mauritius	2009	118	71,705	1.6	0.5	0.3	0.9
Mozambique	2006	4,166	204,847	20.3	6.8	4.1	11.7
Namibia	2010	407	343,241	1.2	0.4	0.2	7.7
Senegal	2010	1,695	287,135	5.9	2.0	1.2	3.4
Sierra Leone	2009	1,196	42,728	28.0	9.3	5.6	16.2
South Africa	2010	7,129	8,321,963	0.9	0.3	0.2	0.6
Swaziland	2010	241	119,548	2.0	0.7	0.4	1.2
Togo	2010	1,287	72,525	17.7	5.9	3.5	10.3
Uganda	2009	8,298	235,649	35.2	11.7	7.0	20.4
Tanzania	2008	8,627	808,012	10.7	3.6	2.1	6.2
Zambia	2007	2,790	86,412	32.3	10.8	6.5	18.7
Median				**10.7**	**3.6**	**2.1**	**6.2**

Source: Data on students and budget provided by UIS upon request. Budget shares computed based on above assumptions.
Note: *Assumptions behind calculations:
(a) Unit price: US$2.00; 5 books per pupil; 1:1 textbook:pupil ratio; book life: 1 year. => Annual per pupil cost: US$**10.00**.
(b) Same as (a) apart from that book life is increased from 1 to 3 years. => Annual per pupil cost: US$**3.30**.
(c) Same as (b) apart from that required textbooks is reduced from 5 to 3. => Annual per pupil cost: US$**2.00**.
(d) Unit and system costs equal medians for grade 1 and 6 for 9 countries surveyed in Read and Bontoux (2013), the R&B Study: Median unit cost: US$3.50; 5 books per grade; 1:1 textbook:pupil ratio and 3-year book life. => Annual per pupil cost: US$**5.80**.

For example, the median share required for the assumptions on which the figures in column 5 are based—$2 per textbook, five books per pupil, one pupil per book, and one-year textbook life—is 10.7 percent. If the average book life is increased from one to three years, the share declines to 3.6 percent. This declines further to 2.0 percent if the number of textbooks required in the grade is reduced from five to three. Finally, 6.2 percent of the budget would be required to meet the median unit and system costs observed in the nine countries surveyed for this study.

The differences between countries are striking. For example, in column 5, the share of budget required (median share of 10.7 percent) ranges from around 1–2 percent in the case of countries with comparatively high gross national product (GNP) per capita—South Africa (0.9 percent), Namibia (1.2 percent), Mauritius (1.6 percent), Botswana (1.8 percent), Cabo Verde (1.8 percent), and Swaziland (2.0 percent)—to 30–35 percent in four low-income countries: Madagascar 30.4 percent, Zambia 32.3 percent, Uganda 35.2 percent, and Guinea 36.3 percent, with the extremes of 50.0 percent for the Central African Republic and 91.7 percent for the Democratic Republic of Congo. These high figures largely reflect a combination of very low per capita income (and thus very low public budgets) and a low share of this income spent on financing public primary education, e.g., Madagascar (1.5 percent of GNP spent on public financing of primary education), Uganda (1.4 percent), the Democratic Republic of Congo (1 percent), Zambia (below 1 percent), and Central African Republic (0.7 percent), all well below the median of 2.3 percent for these 31 countries.

Table 6.4 summarizes the annual per pupil textbook cost resulting from different combination of unit textbook costs and system costs. Columns 1–4 give the results for a textbook:pupil ratio of 1:1, columns 5–8 for a textbook:pupil ratio of 1:2, and columns 9–12 for a textbook:pupil ratio of 1:3. For example, at a unit cost of US$2.00 (the lower end of the US$2–3 unit price range is considered achievable), the annual textbook costs per pupil would range from US$10.00 to US$0.66 depending on the textbook:pupil ratio (1:1, 1:2, or 1:3),

Table 6.4 Annual Textbook Costs per Primary School Pupil for Different Unit and System Costs (US$)

	Textbook:pupil ratio = 1:1				Textbook:pupil ratio = 1:2				Textbook:pupil ratio = 1:3			
	1-year book life		3-year book life		1-year book life		3-year book life		1-year book life		3-year book life	
System costs	5 bks per grade	3 bks per grade	5 bks per grade	3 bks per grade	5 bks per grade	3 bks per grade	5 bks per grade	3 bks per grade	5 bks per grade	3 bks per grade	5 bks per grade	3 bks per grade
Unit costs per textbook:	(1)	(2)	(3)	(4)	(5)	(6)	(7)	(8)	(9)	(10)	(11)	(12)
US$2:00	10.00[a]	6.00	3.30[a]	2.00[a]	5.00	3.00	1.70	1.00	3.30	2.00	1.10	0.66
US$3.50	17.50	10.50	5.80	3.50	8.80	5.30	2.90	1.74	5.80	3.50	1.90	1.14

a. These three annualized per-pupil costs correspond to those on which the budget shares in columns 5, 6, and 7 of table 6.3 are based.

the number of books per grade (three or five books) and the length of book life (one or three years). At a unit price of US$3.50, the corresponding range is from US$17.50 to US$1.14.

Table 6.5 illustrates the share of the primary education budget needed to provide textbooks under the different annual per pupil costs shown in table 6.4. The figures are derived in the same way as those in columns 5–8 of table 6.3: The annual per pupil costs under different assumptions for unit and system cost shown in table 6.4 are, for each of the 30 countries shown in table 6.3, multiplied with the actual enrollment (table 6.3, column 3) and the resulting annual textbook costs is expressed as a percentage of the actual budget (table 6.3, column 4). Thus, the percentages show the share of the primary education budget that the "median" of the 31 countries would need to spend on textbooks according to different unit costs (US$2 and US$3.5) and different system costs.

While these calculations are merely illustrative, they demonstrate the likely range in the share of primary budgets needed to provide textbooks under alternative assumptions for unit textbook costs, system costs, and textbook availability. In particular:

1. The assumptions range from an upper end regarding textbook availability (one book per pupil, five books per grade, one year book life) to a lower end with three pupils sharing one book, three books per grade, and three-year book life. At a unit textbook cost of US$2.00, *the upper end* could be achieved by spending *10.7 percent* of the "median" SSA country's primary education budget on textbooks. (This share would increase if other basic TLM were also included.) The budget share needed to provide five books per grade could be halved to *5.4 percent* if two pupils share one book, or book life were increased from one to two years. The share can be further reduced by increasing further the number of pupils sharing one book and/or the length of book life. At a unit price of US$2.00 and a book life of three years, spending 3.6 percent of the primary

Table 6.5 Share of Primary Education Budget Needed to Provide Textbooks for Different Unit and System Costs (%)

	Book:pupil ratio = 1:1				Book:pupil ratio = 1:2				Book:pupil ratio = 1:3			
	1-year book life		3-year book life		1-year book life		3-year book life		1-year book life		3-year book life	
System costs	5 bks per grade	3 bks per grade	5 bks per grade	3 bks per grade	5 bks per grade	3 bks per grade	5 bks per grade	3 bks per grade	5 bks per grade	3 bks per grade	5 bks per grade	3 bks per grade
Unit costs per textbook:	(1)	(2)	(3)	(4)	(5)	(6)	(7)	(8)	(9)	(10)	(11)	(12)
US$2:00	10.7[a]	6.4	3.6[a]	2.1[a]	5.4	3.2	1.8	1.1	3.6	2.1	1.2	0.7
US$3.50	18.7	11.2	6.2	3.7	9.5	5.6	3.2	1.9	6.3	3.7	2.1	1.2

Note: See explanation in the text. These shares represent the median for the 31 countries listed in table 6.3.
a. These budget shares correspond to the median budget shares in columns 5, 6, and 7 of table 6.3.

education budget would permit providing all pupils with five textbooks in each grade. This is only a little more than *half the median share of 6.6 percent actually spent by the 15 countries* covered in table 6.2. In fact, assuming a book life of three years, the median budget share *actually spent* by these 15 countries should permit the "median country" to provide all pupils with five textbooks in each grade even at a unit price of US$3.50.[9]

2. At a unit textbook cost of US$3.50, the share needed to reach the upper end would increase to *18.7 percent*, which is very high, especially when TLM other than textbooks are included. But even at this unit price, the share can be lowered to 5–6 percent by a combination of increasing the number of pupils per book, increasing book life, and/or decreasing the average number of books needed per grade. At the lowest standard of provision presented in tables 6.4 and 6.5—textbook:pupil ratio of 1:3, three-year book life, and three books per grade—the budget share required is lowered to *0.7 percent* for a unit cost of US$2.00 and *1.2 percent* for a unit cost of US$3.50.

3. No low-income SSA country has reached the upper-end scenario in terms of textbook provision; many may not even have reached the lower end. The share of the budget needed for the "median country" in case it had the unit textbook and system costs of the nine survey countries, leading to a median annual cost per pupil of US$5.80, would be 6.2 percent (see column 8 of table 6.3). The share would be reduced to 3.2 percent if the unit costs could be brought down to US$2.00.

Budget Share Needed for TLM Other Than Textbooks

The above calculations refer to textbooks only. To this should be added other basic TLM such as readers, dictionaries, teacher guides, libraries, and so forth. As already noted, in breaking down the 33 percent of nonsalary recurrent expenditure target of the FTI's Indicative Framework, Rasera (2003) estimated an annualized per pupil textbook cost of US$1.70 for a unit price of US$2.50 per book to reach a "minimum level" of textbook provision (two pupils per book, four books per grade, and a three-year book life). For the median of the 31 countries included in table 6.2, this would mean about 2 percent of the primary education budget. The cost of TLM other than textbooks was estimated by Uythem and Verspoor (2005, table 12.2) (see table 6.6).

Table 6.6 Cost of Teaching and Learning Materials Other than Textbooks

	US$
Dictionary (1 per classroom, 40 pupils, 5-year life):	0.03
Classroom library (40 books per classroom, 10-year life):	0.20
Teacher guides (one guide per teacher in 6 subjects, 7-year life):	0.10
Collective classroom materials (based on UNICEF kit for the Democratic Republic of Congo):	0.90
Total	**1.23**

Source: Uythem and Verspoor 2005 (table 12.2).

Adding this to the cost of textbooks would increase the annual cost for TLM to US$2.93 and raise the annual budget share to about 3.4 percent of the primary education budget.

Summary

The key lesson to be drawn from these illustrations is that, based on the actual budgets in 31 SSA countries and reasonable assumptions about unit cost and book life, *spending 3–5 percent of the primary education budget on textbooks should allow a country to provide all pupils with three to five textbooks per grade.* To this should be an added 1–2 percent of the budget to achieve at least a minimum provision of other TLMs.

Estimated Share of Secondary Education Budget Needed for Adequate Supply of Textbooks

Total Secondary Education

Similar to the analysis for primary education, this section explores the share of the public education budget for *secondary education* that would be required to provide textbooks for all students according to different levels of annualized textbook costs. Table 6.7—covering the 29 countries for which data were available—shows the total number of students enrolled in secondary education (column 3) and the public education budget for total secondary education (column 4) for the corresponding year (largely 2009 or 2010).

Based on these figures, the estimated share of the secondary education budget needed to provide textbooks to all students for different *unit* and *system textbook costs*, leading to different *annual per pupil textbook costs*, is shown in columns 5–8. The last line shows the median budget share for these 29 countries. The share of the education budget needed for textbooks shown is based on the following assumptions:

- **Column 5.** *Unit textbook cost:* US$5, which is the middle of the US$4–6 range for secondary textbook cost suggested possible in the Read and Bontoux (forthcoming) study. *System costs*: Eight books per grade, 1:1 textbook:pupil ratio, and three-year textbook life. This yields an *annual textbook cost per student of* US$13.30. As shown in the last line of the table, at this cost, the median share of the secondary education budget for the 29 countries covered would be *10.0 percent.*

- **Column 6.** Same assumptions as for column 5 except that book life is increased from three to five years. These *system cost* parameters—eight books per grade, textbook:pupil ratio of 1:1, and five-year book life—reflect the corresponding median parameters for grades 8 and 11 in the nine countries surveyed for this study. This yields an annual textbook cost per student of US$8.00. At this cost, the median budget share would be *6.0 percent.*

Table 6.7 Estimated Share of Secondary Education Budget (Recurrent and Capital) Needed to Provide Textbooks for Different Unit and System Costs

Country (1)	Year (2)	Enrollment (000s) (3)	Budget (000s) (4)	Required budget share (%)*			
				(a) (5)	(b) (6)	(c) (7)	(d) (8)
Botswana	2009	180	328,904	0.7	0.4	0.3	1.7
Burkina	2010	538	63,676	11.2	6.8	4.3	10.8
Burundi	2010	338	41,562	10.1	6.1	5.8	9.7
Central African Republic	2010	86	5,740	20.0	12.0	7.5	19.2
Cameroon	2010	1,283	412,766	4.2	2.5	1.6	4.0
Cabo Verde	2009	62	29,952	2.7	1.6	1.0	2.6
Chad	2010	430	57,889	10.0	6.0	3.8	9.6
Congo, Rep.	2010	284	398,380	1.0	0.6	0.4	0.9
Congo, Dem. Rep.	2010	3,484	110,943	41.7	25.1	15.7	40.1
Ethiopia	2010	4,207	132,593	42.2	25.3	15.8	40.6
Gambia, The	2010	124	9,409	17.5	10.5	6.6	16.8
Ghana	2010	1,992	661,668	4.0	2.4	1.5	3.8
Guinea	2008	531	12,888	54.7	33.0	20.6	52.6
Kenya	2006	2,584	300,077	11.5	6.9	4.3	11.1
Lesotho	2008	107	36,292	4.0	2.4	1.5	3.8
Madagascar	2009	1,022	49,541	27.4	16.5	10.3	26.4
Mali	2009	686	154,736	5.8	3.5	2.2	5.6
Mauritius	2009	134	129,907	1.5	0.9	0.6	1.4
Mozambique	2006	368	103,995	4.8	2.9	1.8	4.6
Namibia	2010	170	201,961	1.0	0.6	0.4	0.9
Niger	2010	303	45,432	9.0	5.4	3.4	8.7
Senegal	2010	725	209,687	4.7	2.8	1.8	4.5
Sierra Leone	2009	352	20,616	22.9	13.8	8.6	22.0
South Africa	2010	4,688	6,163,516	1.0	0.6	0.4	0.9
Swaziland	2010	89	90,009	1.3	0.8	0.5	1.2
Togo	2010	460	35,899	17.1	10.3	6.4	16.5
Uganda	2009	1,278	98,786	17.3	10.4	6.5	16.6
Tanzania	2008	1,638	140,131	15.6	9.4	5.9	15.0
Zambia	2007	734	20,951	46.6	28.0	17.5	44.8
Median				**10.0**	**6.0**	**3.8**	**9.6**

Source: Data on students and budget provided by UNESCO Institute for Statistics on request. Budget shares computed based on above assumptions.

Note: * Assumptions behind calculations:
(a) Unit price: US$5.00; 8 books per pupil; 1:1 textbook:pupil ratio; book life: 3 years. => Annualized per pupil cost: US$**13.30**.
(b) Same as (a) apart from that book life is increased from 3 to 5 years. => Annual per pupil cost: US$**8.00**.
(c) Same as (b) apart from that required textbooks is reduced from 8 to 5. => Annual per pupil cost: US$**5.00**.
(d) Unit and system costs equal medians for Grade 8 and 11 for nine countries surveyed in the Read and Bontoux study: Median unit cost: US$8.00; 8 books per grade; 1:1 textbook:pupil ratio and 5-year book life. => Annual per pupil cost: US$**12.80**.

- **Column 7.** Same as column 6 except that the number of required books per grade is reduced from eight to five. This yields an annual cost per student of US$5.00. At this cost, the median budget share would be *3.8 percent*.

- **Columns 8.** Same as system cost parameters as for column 6—i.e., the system costs of the nine countries surveyed for this study—but the unit cost is increased from US$5.00 to US$8.00, which is the unit cost of these nine countries. This yields an annual textbook cost per student of US$12.80. At this cost, the median budget share would be *9.6 percent*.

As with the case for primary education, the median value of the budget share required for each of the above four combinations of unit and system costs varies widely. For example, the median budget share required for the assumptions on which the figures in column 5 are based is 10.0 percent, ranging from below 1.0 percent in the case of countries with comparatively high GDP per capita—Botswana (0.7 percent), Republic of Congo, and Namibia and South Africa (1.0 percent)—to Swaziland (1.3 percent) and Mauritius (1.5 percent), and on to Central African Republic (20 percent) and Guinea (54.7 percent). These variations are caused by similar factors as for primary education. But, in addition, the importance of private and parental contribution to textbook financing is probably higher in secondary than in primary education.

The annual per-pupil textbook costs are summarized in table 6.8 for two different unit costs (US$5.00 and US$8.00), two different textbook:pupil ratios (1:1 and 1:2), and two different assumptions for book life (three years and five years) and the number of books required in each grade.

Table 6.9 shows the resulting *median* shares of the secondary education budget for the 29 countries included in table 6.6 needed to provide for these annualized costs.

While the results of these simulations are merely illustrative, they do suggest the likely range in the share of the actual secondary education budget needed to provide textbooks under alternative reasonable assumptions concerning unit and system costs for the median of the 29 countries shown in table 6.6. In particular:

Table 6.8 Annual Textbook Costs per Secondary School Student for Different Unit and System Costs (US$)

	Book:pupil ratio = 1:1				Book:pupil ratio = 1:2			
	3-year book life		5-year book life		3-year book life		5-year book life	
System costs	8 bks per grade	5 bks per grade	8 bks per grade	5 bks per grade	8 bks per grade	5 bks per grade	8 bks per grade	5 bks per grade
Unit costs per textbook:	(1)	(2)	(3)	(4)	(5)	(6)	(7)	(8)
US$5:00	13.30	8.30	8.00	5.00	6.65	4.15	4.00	2.50
US$8.00	21.30	13.30	12.80	8.00	10.65	6.65	6.40	4.00

Source: Calculated on basis of unit and system cost assumptions provided in the table.

Table 6.9 Share of Secondary Education Budget Needed to Provide Students with Textbooks for Different Unit and System Costs (%)

	Book:pupil ratio = 1:1				Book:pupil ratio = 1:2			
	3-year book life		5-year book life		3-year book life		5-year book life	
System costs	8 bks per grade	5 bks per grade	8 bks per grade	5 bks per grade	8 bks per grade	5 bks per grade	8 bks per grade	5 bks per grade
Unit costs per textbook:	(1)	(2)	(3)	(4)	(5)	(6)	(7)	(8)
US$5:00	10.0a	6.3	6.0a	3.8a	5.0	3.1	3.0	1.9
US$8.00	16.0	10.0	9.6a	6.1	8.0	5.0	4.8	3.0

Source: Calculated on basis of data in tables 6.6 and 6.7.
a. These budget shares correspond to the median budget shares in columns 5–8 in table 6.6.

1. These assumptions range from a high-end provision standard (one book per pupil, eight books per grade, three-year book life) to a low-end with two pupils sharing one book, five books per grade, and five-year book life. For a unit cost of US$8.00 (i.e., the median unit cost in grades 8 and 11 in the nine countries surveyed in Reed and Bontoux forthcoming), this *high end* could be achieved by spending *16.0 percent* of the "median" country's secondary education budget on textbooks. If the unit cost could be lowered to US$5.00, the budget share could be lowered to *10.0 percent*. For the low-end provision standard, *3.0 percent* of the budget would be required for a unit cost of US$8.00 and *1.9 percent* for a unit cost of US$5.00.
2. Similar to that for primary education, the most interesting lesson is that, between the high- and low-end standards, under a number of reasonable assumptions concerning unit and system costs, *by spending 4–6 percent of the secondary education budget on textbooks, the median country could achieve a level of textbook availability much better than what is currently the case.* For example, at the unit cost of $8.00, budget allocation of 6 percent would allow providing five textbooks per pupil in each grade, at a textbook:pupil ratio of 1:1 if a book life of five years could be achieved. On the other hand, for the same budget share, bringing unit cost down to $5.00 would allow increasing the number of textbooks per grade to eight. Naturally, if two pupils were to share one book, these budget shares would be halved.

Comparing the annual per-student costs and budget shares for primary and secondary education shows that they are not all that different though the range is a bit wider for primary than for secondary education. For example, for a textbook:pupil ratio of 1:1, the annual costs range from US$2.00 to US$17.50 for primary education and from US$5.00 to US$21.30 for secondary education. The corresponding budget shares range from 2.2 percent to 18.7 percent for primary education, and from 3.8 percent to 16.0 percent for secondary education. This reflects largely different assumptions about system costs, leading to different annualized per-student costs. In particular, the assumptions for the *upper limit* for book life (three years) and number of books per grade (five) for primary education correspond to the *lower limit* assumptions for secondary education. This reflects the situation in the nine countries surveyed for this study where the median country aimed for five textbooks per grade and a three-year book life in primary education compared with eight books per grade and a five-year book life in secondary education.

Apart from the problems related to cost and financing data availability just discussed, the sections that follow will discuss three other factors affecting the calculations:

1. How does the budget share for secondary education differ between the lower and upper cycles of secondary education ("Budget Shares by Cycle")?
2. How does private education affect the calculated share ("Summary")?
3. How does external aid affect the share ("Impact of External Aid")?

Budget Shares by Cycle

Data were available on secondary school enrollment *and* public education expenditures by cycle for 19 SSA countries for around 2009–10. The median share of total enrollments in the lower secondary cycle was 72 percent. Since both unit and system costs differ by cycle, the budget shares needed to provide textbooks also differ. Similar to that shown above for primary and total secondary education, table 6.10 shows two sets of estimates of the budget shares needed for the median of these 19 countries to provide students in each cycle with textbooks,[10] based on the system and unit costs reported by the nine countries surveyed for this study:

1. The budget shares in the first row of table 6.10 reflect the *median* unit and system costs in total secondary education as well as in each cycle in the nine "survey countries." For the *lower cycle* (grade 8), the median unit textbook cost

Table 6.10 Annual per-Student Book Costs and Budget Shares to Provide Students with Textbooks for Different Unit and System Costs in Secondary Education, Total and by Cycle

	Total secondary education		Lower secondary cycle		Upper secondary cycle	
System costs	Annual per-student cost ($)	Total secondary budget (%)	Annual per student cost ($)	Lower cycle secondary budget (%)	Annual per student cost ($)	Upper cycle secondary budget (%)
Unit costs per textbook: Median in survey countries[a]	12.80[b]	9.6[c]	12.00	10.1	18.40	6.6
$5.00	8.00	6.0	10.00	8.4	8.00	2.9

Note: Share is the median for the 19 SSA countries for which both enrollment and public expenditure data were available by cycle.
a. The medians were US$8 for total secondary education, US$6 for the lower cycle, and US$11.50 for the upper cycle.
b. Corresponds to annual per-student cost in second row, column 3 in table 6.7.
c. Corresponds to budget share in second row, column 3 in table 6.8.

was US$6.00 and the targeted parameters determining system costs were eight books per grade, 1:1 textbook:pupil ratio, and a four-year book life. For the *upper cycle* (grade 11), median unit cost was US$11.50, eight books per grade, 1:1 textbook:pupil ratio, and a five-year book life. For the two cycles combined, the median unit cost was US$8.00, with system costs the same as for the upper cycle.
2. The estimates in second row maintain the above system costs, but the unit book cost is reduced to US$5.00 (the middle of the US$4–6 range).

Table 6.10 shows that, if the "median" country's (i.e., median for the 19 countries) system costs corresponded to those of the median for the nine survey countries, then the following results:

- **For total secondary education**, 9.6 percent of the total budget for secondary education would be required to provide for these system costs if the unit textbook costs also corresponded to the median for the survey countries (US$8.00). The share would be reduced to 6.0 percent if the unit cost could be reduced to US$5.00, i.e., the middle of the US$4–6 unit cost range suggested as possible in the Read and Bontoux (forthcoming) study.[11]
- **For lower secondary education**, the share of the budget would range from 8.4 percent to 10.1 percent depending on the unit cost.
- **For upper secondary education**, the share would range from 2.9 percent to 8.4 percent.

We note the comparatively lower budget share required for the upper than for the lower cycle even in the first case where the unit book cost is almost double in the upper cycle (US$11.50 compared to US$6.00). This is explained by several factors.

1. The assumed *textbook book life* in the lower cycle is four years against five in the upper cycle. Other things being equal, this increases annual per-student book costs in the lower cycle by 20 percent.
2. Public spending per student is higher in the upper cycle. For the 19 countries, the median annual recurrent cost per student was US$127 in the lower cycle and US$278 in the upper cycle. Thus, other things being equal, the textbook cost for the upper cycle as a share of the budget is more than twice that of the lower cycle.[12]
3. Finally, because of paucity of data, the enrollment figures cover public and private education while the budget figures cover only public expenditures. While data on enrollment in private education are available, the corresponding information on funding of private schools is not available. The source of such funding varies considerably by country, ranging from situations where most expenditures of privately managed schools (e.g., by churches) may be government funded to for-profit schools with little or no government support. The median share of private schools in total secondary enrollment in SSA

in 2008 was 15 percent. While data are not available separately for the two cycles, the share is likely higher in the upper than in the lower cycle.

Summary

A key lesson to be drawn from these illustrations is that, based on the actual budgets in 29 SSA countries and reasonable assumptions about unit and system costs, spending 4–6 percent of the secondary education budget on textbooks should allow a country to provide all pupils with five to eight textbooks per grade if the unit costs can be brought down to US$5.00. If a five-year textbook life can be achieved, a budget allocation of about 6 percent would allow providing eight books to all students at a unit book price of US$8.00. The share of the budget needed is higher for the lower than for the upper secondary cycle.

Impact of External Aid

Over the past decades, external aid has played an important role in funding education in many SSA countries. In 2010, SSA received US$3.7 billion (28 percent of all education aid worldwide). About 48 percent of the aid was for basic education. UNESCO (2012, 146) estimates the median share of aid in total government and donor spending on education for the period 2004–10 at about 22 percent for the 27 SSA countries for which data were available. There are, however, very large variations around the median, ranging from practically nil in some countries to over 50 percent in Mozambique and Zambia. Aid has had an impact on textbook provision in SSA in a variety of ways. For example:

Availability. For several decades, donors have been major providers of textbooks in most SSA countries, by providing the books directly, or indirectly by financing countries' book procurement as well as the development, publishing, printing, and/or distribution of textbooks and other TLMs. For example, as noted earlier, 72 percent of the 110 education projects the World Bank financed in 40 SSA countries between 1985 and 2000 included support for textbooks. Many other donors have also provided support for textbooks. In terms of availability, and assuming that suitable textbooks were available on the market, this has been very beneficial, at least in the short term, because large amounts of textbooks could be made available relatively quickly. This has been particularly helpful in rapidly restarting education provision in many countries coming out of conflict.

Financing. It is not known how much of donor funding has been used for textbooks. However, given that most aid has been for nonsalary inputs, the donors' extensive support for textbooks over decades, and the poor progress in establishing sustainable and predictable national textbook funding, it is safe to assume that if aid accounts for 22 percent of the total education budget in the median SSA country, the share of donor funding in the financing of textbooks is much higher.

Textbook costs. As discussed in chapter 5, the important role of donors in textbook provision affects textbook costs in many ways. For example, when aid funding leads to more transparent procurement through competitive bidding, this has in many cases considerably reduced unit textbook cost. Similarly, when aid leads to selection of external publishers, it may reduce cost of printing and raw materials but may also increase overhead and distribution costs.

Capacity building. In addition to funding textbook procurement, aid has also been used to build national capacity in most links of the textbook chain. For example, many World Bank projects have provided such support, ranging from capacity building for prepress work (including for books in national languages) to printing, distribution, and storage. Other donors have provided similar support. But, as illustrated throughout the Reed and Bontoux (forthcoming) study, this support has largely failed to establish the information, planning, management, monitoring, and accountability systems required to successfully address the high cost/low availability textbook problem. There are many reasons for this, including that part of the support focused on creating public sector textbook publishing capacity.[13] Furthermore, the dominant donor role in book provision may also be a key reason for the inadequate attention given by SSA governments to establishing the sustainable systems required to address the problem.

Donor funding is likely to impact the estimated budget shares in different ways. First, to the extent donor financing affects textbook costs, it will affect the annualized cost per student, and thus the budget share. Second, and possibly quite important, it is not known to what extent donor funding is included in the public expenditure data countries report. For some countries, part of this funding may have been included (e.g., if the support is through budget support). In many other cases, textbook funding through investment projects may not have been included. Thus, for some countries, the budget shares calculated in tables 6.3 and 6.6 may reflect the share of textbook funding in *total* domestic and external public education funding; in others, it may reflect only the share in domestic funding.

Finally, education aid increased by 77 percent globally between 2002 and 2010 but only by 38 percent in SSA. The increase slowed toward the end of the period and halted between 2009 and 2010, with a small decline for SSA. It seems safe to assume that the growth in the early part of last decade will not be repeated in the current decade. Therefore, in line with that the single most important recommendation of this report—i.e., the urgent need to establish the sustainable and transparent national systems needed to address the high textbook cost/low textbook availability problem—*aid should give higher priority to supporting the development of such systems* rather than to continue to supply textbooks in an uncoordinated and unpredictable manner.

Although, as noted, aid for capacity building was not very effective in the past, many of the factors that led to this failure are changing, for example, with more reliance on private sector rather than state publishing; more effective and transparent procurement methods; selection of textbooks from government-approved lists, including book price as an important selection criterion; better-qualified national staff; and improved information systems. In addition, given the cost-effectiveness of teaching and learning materials in improving learning outcomes, *the increased global focus on learning must lead to sharply increased efforts to ensure that all pupils have adequate learning materials.* And, as noted elsewhere, while the role of various types of electronic learning materials certainly will rise rapidly, written materials will continue to play a crucial role in SSA, as elsewhere, for many years to come. Countries need to develop the capacity to make judicious decisions on the most cost-effective balance between different types of TLMs, including electronic materials.

Notes

1. This is not only the case for SSA. For example, the background paper for the Philippines (World Bank 2011, para 10) notes, "Frequently, shortage of funding is blamed for the scarcity of textbooks. However, the main problems are often found in other links of the textbook supply chain, or the funds available are not used effectively, or funds are made available on an irregular basis, depending on donor projects. In the Philippines, large amounts of textbooks are procured through World Bank and ABD projects which support the Government's... free textbook policy."
2. This assessment is reiterated in Colclough (1993, 188) who notes, "The first quality-enhancing reform seeks to ensure that, at a minimum, annual expenditures on learning resources equivalent to US$5 per child are made. That is a realistic figure for the majority of developing countries and sufficient to make a considerable impact on school quality when compared with existing levels."
3. World Bank (1988, 141). This is the median for 33 SSA countries.
4. This is the increase in unit cost textbooks per pupil between 2000 and 2015 to reach Education for All program goals necessary to meet basic needs for learning materials. The costs for both years also include "school operating expenditures."
5. World Bank (2002), 14. This corresponded to US$9 per student as a nonweighted average for the 33 SSA.
6. The assumption was that primary education is fee-free and that additional incentives would be provided to overcome demand-side constraints for disadvantaged children (Bruns, Mingat, and Rakotomalala 2003).
7. The US$1.70 estimate for textbooks is based on a unit cost of US$2.50, one book for two pupils in four main subjects and a three-year book life. The "desirable" level of textbooks was costed at US$5.00: Unit cost of US$2.50, one book per pupil in six main subjects and a three-year book life.
8. This is an estimate of the median number of textbooks needed per pupil as an average for all grades, taking into account that a higher share of primary enrollment is in the lower grades where fewer books are needed. The median was four books for grade 1 and seven for grade 6 in the nine countries covered in Read and Bontoux (forthcoming), the R&B Study.
9. Seven of the nine countries covered by Read and Bontoux (2013) are included in table 6.3. Their median budget share to reach this level of provision is 6.5 percent, which is about the same as the actual share for these 15 countries.
10. The median budget shares have been derived in the same way as for primary and total secondary education (see tables 6.3 and 6.6), i.e., country by country, the annualized student cost for each cycle has been multiplied by the enrollment in that cycle and expressed as a percentage of public education expenditures for that cycle. Only the medians are shown here; the results for the individual countries are not shown.

11. These results are the same as those in column 3 of table 6.6 that refer to the same assumptions regarding unit and system costs, but which refer to the median for the 29 countries for which data were available on enrollment and budget for *total* secondary education. Thus, these median shares are the same for the sample of 19 countries as for the larger sample of 29 countries.
12. These unit cost differences by cycle are largely explained by corresponding differences in teacher salaries and pupil-teacher ratios. Data on salary differences are not available. The average pupil-teacher ratio in SSA in 2008 was 31 for lower and 19 for upper secondary education.
13. Box 5.1 summarizes the evolution of the textbook publishing industry in SSA.

References

ADEA (Association for the Development of Education in Africa). 2005. *The Challenge of Learning: Improving the Quality of Basic Education in Sub-Saharan Africa*. Paris: ADEA.

Bruns, B., A. Mingat, and H. Rakotomalala. 2003. *Achieving Universal Primary Education by 2015: A Chance for Every Child*. Washington, DC: World Bank.

Colclough, C., with K. Lewin. 1993. *Educating All the Children: Strategies for Primary Education in the South*. Oxford, UK: Clarendon.

Colclough, C., S. Al-Samarrai, P. Rose, and M. Tembon. 2003. *Achieving Schooling for All: Costs, Commitment, and Gender*. Farnham, UK: Ashgate.

Fredriksen, B. 2009. "Rationale, Issues, and Conditions for Sustaining the Abolition of School Fees." In *Abolition of School Fees in Africa: Lessons from Ethiopia, Ghana, Kenya, Malawi, and Mozambique*, 1–41. Washington, DC: World Bank and UNICEF.

Fredriksen, B., and J. P. Tan, eds. 2008. *An African Exploration of East Asian Education Experience*. Washington, DC: World Bank.

Hallak, J. 1990. *Investing in the Future: Setting Educational Priorities in the Developing World*. Paris: UNESCO.

Rasera, J.-B. 2003. "Le financement d'une éducation de qualité." Background paper prepared for "The Challenge of Learning: Improving the Quality of Education in Sub-Saharan Africa." ADEA, Paris.

Read, A., and V. Bontoux. Forthcoming. *Where Have all the Textbooks Gone? The Affordable and Sustainable Provision of Learning and Teaching Materials in Sub-Saharan Africa*. Washington, DC: World Bank.

UNESCO (United Nations Educational, Scientific, and Cultural Organization). 1998. "Development of Education in Africa: A Statistical Review." MINEDAF VII UNESCO, Paris.

———. 2012. *EFA Global Monitoring Report 2012*. Paris: UNESCO.

UNESCO and UIS (UNESCO Institute for Statistics). 2011. *Financing of Education in Sub-Saharan Africa: Meeting the Challenge of Expansion, Equity, and Quality*. Montreal, Canada: UNESCO and UIS.

UNICEF (United Nations Children's Fund). 2008. "Basic Education and Gender Equality: Essential Learning Package." UNICEF, New York. http://www.unicef.org/education/index_44887.html.

Uythem, B., and Verspoor, A. 2005. "Financing Quality Basic Education." In A. Verspoor, ed, *The Challenge of Learning: Improving the Quality of Basic Education in Sub-Saharan Africa*, 293–321. Paris: Association for the Development of Education in Africa (ADEA).

World Bank. 1988. *Education in Sub-Saharan Africa: Policies for Adjustment, Revitalization, and Expansion*. A World Bank Study. Washington, DC: World Bank.

———. 2002. "World Bank Support for Provision of Textbooks in Sub-Saharan Africa (1985–2000)." Africa Region Human Development Working Paper Series, World Bank, Washington, DC.

———. 2008. "Textbooks and School Library Provision in Secondary Education in Sub-Saharan Africa." Africa Region Human Development Working Paper Series, Working Paper 126, World Bank, Washington, DC.

———. 2011. *Making Textbooks Available to All Students: Barriers and Options. Country Comparator Case Study: Philippines*. Working paper, World Bank, Washington, DC.

World Bank and UNICEF. 2009. *Abolishing School Fees in Africa: Lessons from Ethiopia, Ghana, Kenya, Malawi, and Mozambique*. Washington, DC: World Bank and UNICEF.

CHAPTER 7

Lessons for Sub-Saharan Africa from Countries in Other Regions

To identify areas in the chain of textbook provision where cost efficiencies could be achieved, examinations of the chain, like that done for Sub-Saharan Africa (SSA), were conducted for India, the Philippines, and Vietnam (World Bank 2011a, 2011b, 2011c). These three countries were chosen because of their success in making textbooks affordable to most students. These comparisons were considered important because they could provide policy options for SSA countries to increase textbook availability and affordability.

India, the Philippines, and Vietnam are diverse in size, although all of them have much larger populations than any SSA country except Nigeria. They also have varying political and administrative systems and present interesting case studies on textbook provision. All three have achieved near universal textbook availability in schools.

India

India produces and procures the most textbooks of the three comparator countries. Because the country's central and state governments share responsibilities for education, the provision of textbooks—including their financing—is complex. Many methods are used across states, for different school levels, and for different school types. The National Council of Education Research and Training (NCERT) is the apex body responsible for developing the national curriculum. It also publishes textbooks and teacher guides for schools affiliated with the Central Board of Secondary Education, a national examination body affiliated with almost 9,000 schools of the country's approximately 173,000 recognized secondary schools. Board-affiliated schools follow a common curriculum, use NCERT textbooks, and use the same exams.

State education boards and the State Councils of Education Research and Training (SCERTs) publish their own textbooks based on the national curriculum developed by NCERT. States publish textbooks in their official language (there are 22 constitutionally recognized languages, including English). India's policy is to provide free textbooks to all children through grade 8.

Content Development

NCERT textbooks are designed and developed by the council's relevant subject departments. Many states—particularly union territories, which are under central government administration—also use textbooks developed by NCERT. Other states use NCERT textbooks in combination with others, including their own, while some states rely entirely on their own textbooks. State-level textbooks are prepared and approved by SCERTs. Authors are chosen from panels of subject specialists, and scripts are finalized after consultations with a wide range of stakeholders, often including civil society and NGOs.

Printing

Textbook printing is fragmented in India. NCERT is responsible for printing national-level textbooks, a function that it outsources to printers selected through competitive bidding. States rely on textbook corporations for printing. Smaller states outsource textbook printing to bigger ones.

Financing

India's 2009 Right to Education Act requires that all children ages 6–14—corresponding to grades 1–8, or elementary education—receive a free education. Thus the central and state governments are committed to providing free textbooks to all children enrolled in grades 1–8. In an effort to remove financial barriers to education, Sarv Shiksha Abhiyan, a centrally funded program, defrays the cost of textbooks for families that do not receive them through state programs.[1] The program also covers financing gaps if state funding is insufficient to cover textbooks, especially for girls. Of the program's US$9.9 billion budget for elementary education in 2010–11, just over 3 percent was spent on free textbooks and accounted for about 43 percent of annual spending on those books. But national figures on textbook spending hide significant disparities in state spending, which are linked to enrollments.

Distribution

NCERT textbooks are distributed by 341 organizations. In most states, block resource centers—and in some cases, cluster resource centers—distribute textbooks to schools. Schools usually receive textbooks within a month of the start of the academic year, though longer delays sometimes occur in more populated states. Once textbooks have been distributed, they belong to students. So, when assessing textbook costs, the life of a book is calculated as one year. But some schools, especially where textbook delivery is delayed, retain books at the end of the year for use in subsequent years.

The cost of textbooks per student is US$12.04 for the 18 textbooks required over the primary education cycle (grades 1–5), US$37.08 for the 34 textbooks required for grades 6–10, and US$32.66–US$51.10, depending on the curricular track, for the 10 textbooks required for grades 11–12 (table 7.1). Thus the total textbook cost per student for grades 1–12 is in the range of US$81.78–US$100.22. The total annual cost of free textbook provision for the entire school cycle is estimated at US$1.27 billion, or about 1.7 percent of public education spending in 2010.

The Philippines

In the Philippines until 1995, the Department of Education, Culture, and Sports (now known as DepEd) was responsible for commissioning the development of textbooks, teacher guides, and other learning materials used in public schools. But that year, growing demand from private publishers to engage in the lucrative textbook industry—which accounted for 70 percent of the country's book publishing market—and criticism that textbooks and teaching materials were of higher quality in private than public schools led to a change in textbook policy. That change ended the government monopoly on textbook development. It also lowered the quality of textbooks and raised their costs. By 1998 the textbook:pupil ratio had risen to 8:1 from the reported almost universal availability of books.

The World Bank–financed Third Elementary Education Project introduced international competitive bidding for textbooks, which helped cut their prices by 40 percent. Experiences from textbook provision under this project led to the formulation of the National Textbook Policy in 2004. A footnote to that policy states that based on a 2002 review of textbook procurement, the Bank provided an internal note to DepEd saying that, because of different procurement processes, different titles for the same grades were purchased in different years

Table 7.1 India: Cost of Textbooks per Pupil and Set of Textbooks by Grade, 2011

Grade	Number of core subjects	Subjects	Unit cost per pupil per grade for each set of textbooks (US$)	Average unit cost per textbook (US$)
1–2	3	Hindi, English, Math	2.00	0.67
3–5	4	Hindi, English, Math, Environmental Science	2.68	0.67
6–8	6	Hindi, English, Math, Science, Social Science, Sanskrit	6.33–6.66	1.06–1.11
9–10	8	Hindi, English, Math, Science, History, Democratic Politics, Economics, Geography	8.88	1.11
11–12	5-Science	Physics, Chemistry, Biology, English, Math	17.75	3.55
	5-Arts	Politics, Economics, Psychology, Sociology, English	25.55	5.11
	5-Commerce	Accountancy, Business Studies, English, Economics, Math	16.33	3.27

Source: NCERT Publications Division 2011.
Note: These costs refer only to textbooks developed by NCERT. In grades 11 and 12, students can opt for any one of the three streams of study: Science, Commerce, and Arts.

and distributed to schools.[2] This problem was compounded by purchases by local school boards of a wide range of titles.

The situation with multiple titles led to a paradox: while there are enough textbooks to meet the desired 1:1 ratio of textbook:pupil, teachers chose only one title (on average) and used it, keeping the other titles for the same subject in storage or in the library as "reference material." Hence the textbook:pupil ratio is less than 1:1. The 2004 National Textbook Policy sought to provide one textbook per pupil in all elementary and secondary public schools nationwide—provided that this would be the minimum, with the same titles used for every subject in every class and school. The policy further clarified that DepEd would provide a single title per subject per grade level in schools within regions so that teachers could use the same instructional materials each year.

Content Development

Until 1995 the Department of Education, Culture, and Sports Department was responsible for developing textbooks and teacher manuals used in public schools. When the textbook industry was opened to private participation, private publishers began developing textbooks by contracting experts accredited by civil society organizations and NGOs as the editorial staff—usually professors from reputable universities. The DepEd is responsible for evaluating textbooks. Publishers must pay all copyright fees to content developers and retain copyrights prior to procurement. The DepEd takes over the right to reprint materials four years after contract awards by paying copyright fees to publishers and royalties to authors. But copyright fees account for only about 1 percent of textbook production costs; most costs involve printing and delivery.

Printing

Private publishers are responsible for printing textbooks. The Instruction Materials Council (under the DepEd) is responsible for quality control. Competition among printers, including international printers, has helped cut textbook costs.

Financing

The national government finances textbook costs under its policy of free provision. Donors—including the World Bank, Asian Development Bank, and AusAid—have also made large contributions to textbook provision. Using a textbook:pupil ratio of 1:1, the annual cost of providing textbooks is estimated at US$63 million for the primary level and US$55 million for secondary, using 2010 costs and enrollment figures (see table 7.2). Another US$3 million is spent each year on teacher guides and manuals. The government's policy of free textbook provision is heavily dependent on donor funding. In 2013 the Department of Education allocated just 0.5 percent of its budget to textbooks. But the scarcity of books reported by schools, with erratic funding cited as a cause, bring into question the financial sustainability of the free textbook policy at a 1:1 textbook:pupil ratio.

Table 7.2 The Philippines: Cost of Textbooks per Pupil per Set of Textbooks by Grade

Grade	Number of textbooks required per pupil per grade	Unit cost per pupil per grade for each set of textbooks (US$)	Average cost of textbook (US$)
1–2	4	3.68	0.92
3–6	6	5.53	0.92
7–10	9	9.99	1.11

Source: DFID Bilateral Support to Primary Education, National Audit Office, 2010.

Procurement

The DepEd's National Bids and Awards Committee procures textbooks. The government follows a parallel but complementary process for procuring textbooks using its own and donor resources. Government procurement occurs through national competitive bidding. Procurement financed by donors occurs through international competitive bidding. Regions procure textbooks every five years for the entire student population for each subject following a published procurement schedule. Thus publishers must have the whole set of textbooks and teacher guides for every subject for all grades ready prior to the start of the procurement process. The procurement cycle, based on each book's lifespan, will be five years. Books are given to students for each academic year and collected at year's end for reuse the following year.

Distribution

The government follows a complex system for textbook delivery. Suppliers are responsible for delivering books to schools. The DepEd has a nationwide partnership with the Consortium of Civil Society Organizations under which representatives of the organizations work with school inspection teams to enforce procedures for delivery and quality control.

Vietnam

As in India, in Vietnam too responsibilities for education are split between the national and provincial levels. The Ministry of Education and Training directly manages only about 5 percent of the education budget; the rest is channeled to provincial people's councils. The councils have full authority to set priorities and allocate education budgets accordingly. But the national government maintains a highly centralized system of textbook provision through the ministry and the Education Publishing House, with the ministry having full authority over all aspects of textbook development, production, and distribution.

Vietnam produces textbooks based on the assumption of a 1:1 ratio of textbooks:pupils and a textbook lifespan of four years. But high annual textbook production indicates that the real life of a textbook is less than four years. That may be partly due to frequent curriculum revisions. Moreover, parents are responsible for providing current and updated textbooks for their children. So although there is a used textbook market and schools sometimes retain used textbooks that are supplied free of cost to some types of students, lack of systematic access to used textbooks might also explain this shortcoming.

Content Development
Textbook authors are chosen by the Education Publishing House and MOET's Council of Subjects and approved by the ministry. They are usually provided by the publishing house or the Educational Sciences National Institute. The government holds the copyrights to all education materials.

Printing
The Education Publishing House controls every aspect of textbook printing. It sources the paper and provides it to printing houses, which charge the publishing house for printing and nonpaper raw materials like ink, glue, zinc, and thread. Any increase in the cost of paper affects the price of textbooks, which have been rising in recent years. Thus the analysis here assumes that the bulk purchasing of paper by the Education Publishing House helps lower costs.

Financing
The national government finances all textbook costs. The allocation of funds is highly centralized, and access to this information is highly restricted. Parents are expected to provide all required textbooks for their children, while the government provides textbooks and learning materials for free or at a reduced price for students in particularly difficult circumstances and students in highland and remote areas. Retail sales cover about three-quarters of textbook costs; government subsidies cover the rest. But these estimates are based on assumptions that cannot be verified for lack of official data on production costs. (For more information, see table 7.3.)

Distribution
The Education Publishing House is responsible for text distribution, and there is a nationwide distribution network. Flexible distribution mechanisms are used. Free textbooks are distributed by provincial books and educational equipment companies (every province has one) or directly to schools, depending on the grade level. Various methods are used to get textbooks to students who must buy

Table 7.3 Vietnam: Cost of Textbooks per Pupil per Set of Textbooks by Grade

Grade	Number of textbooks required per pupil per grade	Unit cost per pupil per grade for each set of textbooks (US$)	Average unit cost per textbook (US$)
1–3	5	4.2	0.8
4–5	9	6.3	0.7
6–7	14	11.2	0.8
8–9	14	14.0	1.0
10–12	13	16.9	1.3

Source: Education Publishing House (2011 data).

their own: they can buy books through retail booksellers, get them from district offices, or buy them directly from publishers.

Concerns have been expressed about the cost and efficiency of Vietnam's textbook production and distribution system. But the low retail costs of textbooks—unless those costs are more heavily subsidized than suggested by the limited official data—actually suggest that textbook production is cheap and efficient.

Summary

India, the Philippines, and Vietnam have ambitious policies and elaborate administrative and management structures for providing textbooks. They have also committed considerable funds to free textbook provision. Each country's government plays a leading in textbook provision, from content development to printing and distribution. In all three countries, books are developed to follow national curriculums, and a single textbook is prescribed for each subject. In India and Vietnam, the ministries of education are responsible for developing textbooks using pools of pre-identified authors. In both countries, copyright is retained by the central governments, lowering reprinting costs. The Philippines uses public-private partnerships, although that setup does not seem to provide any quality advantages.

Having achieved the ambitious targets of textbooks for all children, the main challenges for all three countries are to improve the quality of textbooks, keep them affordable, and make financing sustainable. As noted earlier in this study, the cost of textbooks with an expected year-long shelf life is about half that of books with shelf lives of four years. In Vietnam a four-year shelf life does not mean much because most students must buy their own books. Better textbook management by schools could significantly lower textbook costs, and the savings could be used to improve quality and lengthen shelf life. Doing so would also lower costs of annual printing, procurement, and distribution—easing pressure on education budgets.

Several elements help keep textbook costs low in India, Vietnam, and the Philippines:

- One standard textbook is provided for each subject.
- Textbooks are written to align with national curriculums.
- The number of textbooks required per grade is closer to the median for SSA countries in the Philippines, slightly higher in Vietnam, and lower in India.
- National governments are responsible for content development (except in the Philippines, where it is contracted to private publishers).
- India and Vietnam retain full copyrights, making reprinting cheaper. The Philippines retains the right to reprint for its five-year textbook procurement cycle.
- India keeps costs low through competitive bidding among approved printers, the Philippines through national competitive bidding—but linking printing and content development costs—and Vietnam by using state printing houses.

Notes

1. About 10 percent of the funding for Sarv Shiksha Abhiyan is external; the rest comes from the central government. In 2004, 2 percent of central taxes went to the primary education budget. That tax was raised to 3 percent in 2008, with the additional 1 percentage point used to finance expansion of secondary and higher education.
2. Similar situations have been reported from other countries (Romania, Uganda), with contradictory experiences. In the Indian state of Tamil Nadu, multichoice textbook policy is a dilemma—but for different reasons. A court case is under way to apply a common curriculum and have different types of schools use the same textbooks, with the goal of setting uniform standards.

References

World Bank. 2011a. "Making Textbooks Available to All Students: Barriers and Options. Country Comparator Case Study: India." Working paper, World Bank, Washington, DC.

———. 2011b. "Making Textbooks Available to All Students: Barriers and Options. Country Comparator Case Study: Philippines." Working paper, World Bank, Washington, DC.

———. 2011c. "Making Textbooks Available to All Students: Barriers and Options. Country Comparator Case Study: Vietnam." Working paper, World Bank, Washington, DC.

CHAPTER 8

Digital Teaching and Learning Materials: Opportunities, Options, and Issues

Predictions about the Demise of Printed Textbooks

Despite regular proclamations about the impending "death of the printed book," printed textbooks—especially in Sub-Saharan Africa (SSA)—aren't going away any time soon. New emerging information and communication technologies (ICTs) rarely fully replace existing technologies, but rather coexist with them in some way.[1] That said, the business climate for "educational publishers" is changing radically everywhere. This change is being fueled by the increased distribution and adoption of a variety of disruptive new technologies, increasingly to be found across the continent in schools and local communities, even some of the poorest. The technology of the printed textbook most likely still has many decades of life and relevance for education systems across SSA. Whether or not the "death of textbooks" happens in the next five, ten, or fifty years, considering only printed textbooks when making long-term decisions about teaching and learning materials (TLM) in SSA may be short-sighted. *The primacy of the printed textbook as the primary method of conveying written material in schools will be increasingly under threat—as it already is in some other parts of the world—by the continued emergence and increased diffusion of electronic and digital technologies.*

Educational Materials and Electronic Devices: Promise and Potential

Across SSA, a variety of devices are increasingly being used to disseminate TLM in electronic and digital formats. As costs continue to fall, and the devices become more widely available and used across communities, the small largely NGO-led pilot projects that have characterized most efforts to introduce

---

Michael Trucano wrote this chapter.

educational technologies in schools across SSA will inevitably be complemented, and in many cases superseded, by national initiatives to distribute hundreds of thousands of electronic devices such as those in Rwanda and Kenya.[2,3]

The use of such devices has great promise and potential to improve the access to and quality of education by providing access to more educational content than is currently available to students. Internet connectivity can provide access to vast quantities of educational materials. Low cost, hand-held e-reading devices can hold more than a thousand books.[4] Depending on connectivity, or local resourcefulness in transferring materials to devices manually, digital content can be updated more regularly than printed materials. Depending on the device used, digital content can be presented as "rich media," with audio, video, and animations helping content to be displayed in engaging and interactive ways. Depending on the technologies employed, the use of content can be presented to teachers and learners in personalized ways and its use tracked. In some cases, content can be delivered at lower costs than traditional printed materials. (But this is certainly not true in all cases. Please see the sections on "Some Common Myths and Misconceptions" and "Costs," which follow.)

Devices Used to Access Digital Educational Content

While most SSA countries have introduced school computer labs for many years, and many large-scale initiatives to do so are being planned, a number of factors—including large upfront costs, maintenance challenges, low utilization for core educational subjects, and the emergence of low-cost portable computing devices—suggest that computer labs will not be a primary venue for the use of digital TLM. Instead, laptops, tablets, and dedicated e-reading devices (e-readers) are more likely to be used to access electronic learning content. While currently not considered a technology of widespread applicability in education systems in SSA—some education systems ban their use—the increased availability of mobile phones also offers a viable technical option for the distribution and use of digital learning content of various sorts. Older, established technologies like radio and television will continue to be used for distributing educational materials to large numbers of learners, especially in remote communities, for many years to come and new devices will continue to emerge as well. As gadgets and digital technologies proliferate, and costs of end-user devices fall, it is likely that greater value will be placed on the content and how it is used rather than on any particular device. *Viewed from this perspective, the future of education is in the content, not the "container."*

Some Common Myths and Misconceptions

Given the increased availability and diffusion of consumer computing technologies across much of SSA in recent years, it is not surprising that widespread misconceptions have taken hold about the potential of using digital technologies across SSA to increase access to learning materials. This is consistent with the "hype cycle" model of technology diffusion in which, according to

Gartner, a technology breakthrough is soon followed by a period of time of "inflated expectations" about of the changes possible as a result.[5] Some of the most common myths and misconceptions of this sort are addressed in the following sections.

"We Will Cut Costs by Going Digital."

The falling costs of devices such as e-book readers are cited as a reason to be optimistic about the potential for the widespread adoption of e-readers in schools in SSA.[6] Although the costs of end-user devices will continue to fall, such costs may in the end represent only a fraction of the overall costs of providing access to digital TLM, which also include things like content distribution (including connectivity), digital content production, and ongoing support and maintenance.[7] Where a country is not already home to a vibrant ecosystem of diverse companies and actors which can enable and support the quick diffusion and use of a particular technology for education purposes—and, outside of perhaps South Africa, no African country has a mature ecosystem of this sort already in place—this ecosystem may need to be developed.

"The Content We Need Is Already Available—and Free."

There is a lot of educational content in digital formats available for potential use without charge.[8] But even where such content is "free," there are many costs associated with making it available to teachers and students. This content needs to be identified. It will need to be vetted for accuracy and appropriateness and possibly contextualized for use within a given educational system. The content may also need to be mapped against existing curricular objectives and presented in such a way that the correspondence between individual content items and a given curriculum are clear to teachers and students. Additional content may be required to fill any gaps and may need to be presented in ways that are user friendly. Teachers may need to be trained in the use of such content and supported over time. In addition, the content itself will need to be distributed to devices. Where this distribution cannot be done digitally—i.e., where there is inadequate or no connectivity—other means will need to be employed. Where digital distribution is technically possible because of the existence of adequate connectivity, investments in content management and distribution systems may still be required.

"If We Don't Act Now, We Will Fall Behind."

One common argument in favor of digital TLM is that education systems that do not embrace the use of technology will suffer in comparison to those that do, and the competitiveness of countries may erode over time as a result. This rhetoric is often invoked by politicians to garner support for related initiatives—aided no doubt by vendors eager to provide "solutions" to "problems" that a country has, in some cases, neither defined nor understood. Thus there is a danger that such concerns can lead to hasty, ill-conceived, or inadequately considered plans to introduce new technologies in schools.

Decisions to introduce digital TLM should not be taken lightly, or quickly. Even where such technologies may be unaffordable, digital TLM are worth considering as part of medium- or long term-planning in all countries across the continent. New technologies offer new opportunities to provide access to teaching and learning resources that were not previously available, sometimes at costs lower than for traditional materials. *But no matter how attractive it may be to leapfrog ahead in adopting and integrating new technologies, it is also possible to leapfrog in the wrong direction.*

"Digital Learning Materials Will Engage and Motivate Our Children."

The rationale for advocating the use of digital TLM is that they are naturally motivating for students, and so will improve learning. The research is decidedly mixed on the extent to which digital materials motivate students to learn and the extent to which this motivation results in better learning outcomes. The devil is in the details here. Some content may motivate learners and some approaches to the use of this content by teachers may motivate learners—and others may not. It is a matter of debate to what extent young people, although living in an increasingly digital world, naturally understand how to integrate the use of technology as part of their learning.[9]

"E-books Can Simply Replace Textbooks."

Although digital textbooks may eventually largely replace printed textbooks, this transition will take many years. In OECD countries where digital learning materials are already in widespread use, traditional printed textbooks are still used extensively (see, for example, OECD 2009). This suggests that, for an indeterminate period of time, even in countries best-equipped for the transition to the use of digital TLM at a wide scale, substituting printed materials with digital ones will not be viable in the near term.

Costs

Calculating costs associated with the introduction of digital TLM is a challenging task. At a basic level, how much a country spends on digital TLM will depend on what it intends to do and its capacity to support such use. In comparison to standard textbook procurement, costing exercises for digital TLM can be challenging and complex. Costs associated with piloting a discrete digital educational materials initiative do not easily correlate with the costs of such a project at scale. Simple projections of costs based on experiences with pilot projects may result in inaccurate calculations—potentially wildly so. In some cases, costs of certain project components should be expected to decrease at scale as a result of various economies of scale inherent in things like the bulk purchasing of goods (textbooks, computers, and so forth) or services (technical support, bandwidth). Other cost components—such as the need for increased coordination, expenses associated with meeting the needs of students with special needs, and the need to revamp existing policies and procedures—may emerge only when a project to introduce digital TLM is pursued at scale. That said, when attempting to identify and quantify such costs, it may be helpful to consider grouping them into three broad components. The first two components—the cost of the *content* and the costs related to *hardware* necessary to use the content—are commonly, if often incompletely, considered. A third cost—related to development and sustaining a necessary *ecosystem* to support the use of digital TLM—is important but often does not factor into the cost calculations. Also, specific costs may vary widely by market and jurisdiction.

In general, methodologies which can help identify, estimate, and compute *total cost of ownership/operation* over time, and not just upfront capital costs, should be used when attempting to estimate and quantify costs related to the procurement and use of digital TLM.

Content-Related Costs

At first glance, buying a digital textbook may seem much like buying a printed textbook, but there can be important differences. Vendors may offer content in a variety of ways.

- It may be sold for use over a given period of time or in perpetuity.
- It may be offered for sale separate from the related intellectual property (IP) rights (as is typical), may be made available under joint IP (less common, more expensive), or the IP may be transferred to the education system outright (rare, unless mandated by government, and expensive).
- It may be offered as a subscription service.
- A vendor may propose to offset certain costs through the use of embedded advertising.
- It may be bundled with other goods or services. For example, content and devices may be sold (or leased) together, with an agreed level of technical support and maintenance. A vendor may offer to provide related training (e.g., for teachers or technical support personal).
- A vendor may offer to sell or lease the content embedded within a larger digital content or learning management system (typically referred to as a CMS or an LMS). It may offer to host the content on its own servers or offer to embed an education system's existing digital content into this CMS. (Where a vendor provides not only content itself but a CMS or LMS as well, it may or may not make available the source code of this CMS or offer a migration path if a country decides to move the content to another CMS. Associated costs for this need to be considered as well.)

A country may want to develop digital teaching and learning content itself by expanding its existing in-house capacity. Costs associated with this approach vary widely, based on the context. Experience also shows that quality may vary widely as well.

Many SSA countries are increasingly considering the use of "free content," especially so-called open educational resources made available for use and reuse without cost.

- Where "free" educational content is used, the cost of the acquisition of the rights to use the content is zero.
- Some countries consider, in part, the use of user-generated content, that is, content created by teachers and students themselves. In such cases, initial acquisition costs may be quite low, provided the capacity exists for teachers and students to develop this content. Where the capacity does not exist, investments may be needed for training and for facilities to develop the content. Also, clear policies and guidelines will be needed for relevant IP. For example: Is it owned by the government or by the creator with free usage rights granted for education purposes?

Regardless of how content is acquired, there may be additional costs related to the following:

- **Vetting** the content for accuracy; appropriateness to local contexts, customs, and cultural mores; and its relevance to existing curricula.
- **Contextualizing** the content as appropriate or necessary.
- **Embedding** the content within a country's education system's existing CMS or LMS.
- **Classifying** or tagging individual content items according to a given metadata scheme, to signify ownership, usage rights, links to curricular objectives, data formats, content types (e.g., text, image, audio, and video), and so forth.
- **Distributing the material**, whether physical, digital, or a combination of the two, and inventory management.

These costs will be in addition to the cost of traditional printed materials in cases where digital materials are not meant to fully replace printed materials.

Device-Related Costs

One cost that is well understood is that of the end-user device on which digital teaching TLM are used, together with the necessary supporting technical infrastructure. This cost includes projected useful life of the device itself; the need for equipment repair, maintenance, and replacement; and non-content-related software purchases and upgrades. There are also costs related to the distribution of the devices and, often, training for end users. There may also be additional costs for maintaining a baseline level of electricity to ensure that the devices can operate. Where there is no reliable access to electricity, cost of local generators and/or solar chargers may need to be considered.

Ecosystem-Related Costs

In addition to costs related to digital TLM themselves, and the devices on which they are to be used, there are a number of costs related to the environment

Digital Teaching and Learning Materials: Opportunities, Options, and Issues

(or "ecosystem") in which such use occurs. These costs can be negligible or considerable, depending on the context and the technologies employed.

- Textbooks have little impact on the budget for school infrastructure. Not so for digital TLMs. School infrastructure may need to be improved to ensure adequate climate control (proper temperature, humidity, and dust levels), adequate physical security, and electrical capacity. Rooms may need to be reconfigured and additional furniture (charging stations, etc.) may be needed.
- At a system level, coordination of initiatives for the use of digital TLM across ministries, and with various actors and stakeholder groups outside government—civil society, academia, and the private sector—will entail additional costs. Costs may also be incurred for national or regional information dissemination campaigns, training, and outreach activities (including for school principals and local community groups), and enhancing connectivity and electricity availability. More fundamental in some cases—and often overlooked in many developing countries—is the need for a vibrant set of local actors who can provide related products, services, and support. The existence of healthy and competitive local publishing and technology industries, for example, may be a key prerequisite for success if the use of digital TLM is to become integral to a country's education system. Digital TLM at scale may need policies, guidelines, laws, and regulations to be formulated, or reformulated, especially with regard to data security and privacy.
- Some system-level or ecosystem costs may traditionally lie outside the purview or responsibility of ministries of education but still need to be taken into account.

One Way to Begin: Targeting Different Age Groups or School Subjects

Countries considering use of digital TLM for the first time may first wish to target a specific cohort of students and/or subjects. Even where countries have decided to take a "big bang approach" to the use of digital TLM across their entire education system (such as the case in the Republic of Korea [Trucano 2011] and Uruguay),[10] they typically adopt a phased approach. By limiting initial efforts to a specific subject (e.g., math or science) or grade level (e.g., primary, middle, or secondary school students), ministries of education can make targeted use of scarce resources while at the same time learning how to implement initiatives featuring digital TLM before expanding them more widely.

Age Groups
There is no consensus on which age levels are the "best" target areas or audiences for the use of digital TLM. The research base offers little guidance in this regard, but some observations about conventional practices may be useful.

- Many investments in digital TLM have targeted students at the upper primary and lower secondary level, because students in this age cohort are literate and

often do not have pressures related to high stakes exams as students at the upper secondary level do.
- Increasingly, investments are being made to provide access to digital TLM in early primary grades, especially where content is highly visual and interactive, such as animations and games. At the primary school level, especially in classrooms with large numbers of students, investments in digital TLM and digital projectors is often seen as a cost-effective way to amortize investments in computer hardware over the widest number of students.
- At the upper secondary level, many countries may opt to invest in digital TLM that directly support exam preparation.

School Subjects

Digital TMLs are used in all academic subjects. Decisions about the potential usefulness of digital content, compared with the use of printed materials, depend on specific educational contexts, needs, and goals.

Digital TLMs are often seen as good candidates in *science, technology, engineering, and mathematics* as their content requires the least amount of customization for use in different countries. Many concepts taught and learned during the course of STEM studies lend themselves well to animated simulations, something that digital TLMs are particularly well suited to include.

- Many initial investments in digital TLM target *language arts* subjects, where teachers have greater scope to incorporate additional or complementary education content into their lesson plans.
- Existing digital educational content in *humanities* subjects, especially in topics like geography and history, requires greater customization than content in science subjects for it to be culturally or politically appropriate in countries other than for which it was initially developed.

Whatever the age cohort or academic discipline, there is strong evidence about the potential utility of digital TLM for students with special educational needs, especially when compared with traditional printed materials supported by traditional pedagogical practices.

Links to Education Reform Processes

The introduction of new digital TLM may be part of a country's larger education reform process. In countries where an education reform process is under way or planned, the introduction of digital TLM can be a valuable tool to help enable and support this change process.

General Trends

The process to "go digital" will be more challenging in SSA than many optimists—some of whom have financial stakes in this transition—would have us believe. While there can be disagreement about the pace of change that is viable and appropriate, some general trends related to the adoption of digital TLM are evident.

The educational publishing industry is changing rapidly around the world, in response to the potential and threats presented by the diffusion of new technologies. Digital transmission of educational content offers near-instantaneous access to almost unfathomable amounts of information via the Internet and other mechanisms, and there is no reason to assume that publishers in SSA will not be affected by these changes. Big international educational publishers are changing their product offerings and going increasingly digital, being forced to adopt new business models along the way.

Communities across SSA have been coming into the digital age. Bandwidth is improving and becoming cheaper and more accessible across the continent. The growth of mobile phones in Africa (in 2012 there were over 650 million mobile phone subscriptions across the continent, rising from almost zero at the turn of the century) is perhaps the most remarkable example of the diffusion of a new information and communication technology in history.

New approaches are being piloted and explored by traditional and new publishers alike. These include new devices (e.g., e-readers), new approaches to IP (e.g., Creative Commons, open educational resources), new opportunities to create and share "user-generated content," and new business models (pay as you go, advertiser-supported, "freemium" content). It is difficult to predict which of these will succeed, but the ones that do may radically change the scope of what is not only possible, but probable.

The concept of a textbook itself is changing. A textbook is a collection of printed pages, officially endorsed, which delineate a linear path through a prescribed set of curricular objectives in a way that cannot easily be changed, along which all students are meant to process at a common pace. The digitization of education materials, and the increased dispersion of technologies and tools to enable the creation, curation, and use of such materials, potentially disrupts each component of such a definition. Many advocates of e-textbooks conceive of them as the electronic version of a traditional printed textbook made available on a technology device, perhaps enlivened by the use of animations and other rich media (audio, video) in ways not possible on a printed page. More radical advocates for e-textbooks stress the potential to curate digital educational content from multiple sources into a "textbook" offering more personalized content presentation to students, based on their own particular learning needs.

The Way Forward: Some Questions and Issues for Consideration

Given the rapid changes in technology, their limited reach in some SSA countries, and the complexity of integrating them in the education systems, there is the risk of making big mistakes while embarking on long-term TLM policies. Some countries are considering cutting textbook budgets, using the budgets instead to buy electronic devises. Others think it is premature to address use of digital TLM in any strategic way. Most countries find themselves in a state of movement somewhere between these two viewpoints.

- Despite the primacy of the printed textbooks across SSA, to what extent should policymakers be exploring options to introduce digital TLM?
- Is there a danger that, in trying to solve the acute challenge of the lack of affordable textbooks for students, policymakers may end up making choices that are to some extent backward-looking, which do not take into account the potential—and perhaps related perils—of technological advances to reshape not only what can be done today but also what might be possible tomorrow?

Answers to these questions will determine the way educational materials are conceived, procured, delivered, and consumed in schools across SSA Africa in coming years. Although answers to the above questions may involve an uncomfortable level of speculation, there are general considerations that can be useful when planning ways to reduce the costs and increase the availability of digital TLM in SSA.

Intellectual property issues will become increasingly complicated—and important. The digitization of learning materials, together with the proliferation of "alternative" approaches to licenses for various type of digital content (like Creative Commons, which has helped spawn the Open Education Resources [OER] movement), is challenging many countries to rethink approaches to educational content. Once content is digitized and made widely available, stealing it becomes much easier. This phenomenon has brought about a radical restructuring of the music industry; the movie and "video" businesses are currently being reshaped by it; and the educational publishing industry is beginning to feel its effects as well. Piracy has of course always occurred. Incidents where countries "buy" textbooks from publishers and then just print more copies as if they own the content itself are not unknown. Piracy can become much more acute when content is digitized, connectivity enables this content to be distributed in the blink of an eye, and an explosion of low-cost end-user devices make accessing and reading such content as easy as flipping a switch or pressing a few buttons. Some countries (such as Indonesia and Poland) are beginning to mandate that publishers make their printed content available for free in digital versions, and others are considering a variety of alternative approaches to IP and publishing as a result, but IP issues are likely to remain complicated. Lack of attention to IP issues in some markets may inhibit incentives for groups to produce high-quality educational content.

The "open educational resources" movement is changing the way educational materials are created—and used. The past decade has seen an explosion of interest and activity in promoting and utilizing OER, which are—in the words of the Hewlett Foundation, which through its grants has been a key supporter and enabler of related activities—"in the public domain or have been released under an IP license that permits their free use or re-purposing by others." The OER movement, which has been made possible by the rapid diffusion of ICTs, challenges traditional approaches to the production, procurement, and use of educational materials. In an age where OER is increasingly being incorporated into national educational portals and where open access is increasingly a larger priority for many governments and educational institutions, issues related to open content may become increasingly central to the procurement and use of learning resources, including textbooks.

Educational content and assessment may become more closely linked. With the disruption of the traditional educational publishing business, certain types of learning content are seen as commodities in certain quarters because they are available "for free." In this scenario, closely anchoring educational content within an assessment platform or tool might make compelling business sense for many educational content providers. Some publishers believe this makes it more difficult to pirate and then market an assessment engine or platform than it is to copy and redistribute education content that someone else has created.[11] Thus, the "textbook industry" may evolve from one which essentially offers products (printed textbooks) to one which offers a menu of related services (including access to digital educational content, assessment tools and services, etc.), further complicating, if not rendering moot, many traditional approaches to textbook procurement.

The lines between the delivery of educational content, including textbooks, and the devices or technologies on which such content is used, may continue to blur. Just as issues related to content and assessment are becoming more closely linked, the lines between content and the hardware and software that enable the use of such content are also blurring. As countries seek to "computerize" their schools on a large scale for the first time, they often ignore just what educational content will be accessed and used (and created) on such devices. In some countries, there are very real worries that purchases of hardware may divert budgets needed to purchase TLM—at least in the short run. Meanwhile, the very nature of textbooks is changing in some places. An example often cited is the "flexbook,"[12] an initiative under which educators can create a textbook in line with the national curriculum by picking and choosing from a lot of assembled educational content. Content developed for a specific device may not be usable at all on another device, leading to potential dependencies on certain hardware and increasing the danger of vendor lock-in in ways that do not affect printed textbooks.

New tools and approaches to creating and using digital educational content also create new opportunities for greater equity, while at the same time erecting some even higher barriers for access to such materials. Many SSA countries are still struggling to provide printed textbooks for all students. Distributing digital content to schools and communities in rural areas, where Internet or 3G connectivity may be poor (or nonexistent or too expensive), access to reliable electricity may be even more problematic, and maintaining the devices may be difficult. As a result, many of the pilot efforts across SSA to date to provide access to digital TLM have been in more urban and more affluent communities, where such challenges are comparatively smaller, creating digital divides and furthering inequities related to socioeconomic status, gender, language, and special educational needs.

Procurement decisions can promote—or inhibit—the development of competitive, innovative, sustainable local digital educational publishing industries. In many SSA countries, educational publishing makes up over 90 percent of the overall publishing market. In places where disposable income is at a premium, and where the culture of buying books is not well-ingrained, the health of the local publishing industry depends largely on textbook procurement. To the extent that one believes that education systems—or more broadly, opportunities for personal learning and growth in general—are well-served by having vibrant, dynamic local publishing markets, it is worth considering how textbook procurement impacts these markets. There are potentially some very real tensions in many places between the desire for countries to acquire TLM at the lowest price per pupil while also promoting the development of competitive local publishing systems. Does lowest cost in the short run equate to lowest cost in the long run? Such a question becomes more important in case of digital as TLM where issues of vendor and/or technology lock-in can be very acute, especially where countries choose "solutions" that rely on proprietary standards and technologies. For example, increased adoption of digital TLM may reduce demand for printed textbooks. This will affect the publishers who may be relying on the large textbook procurements for their survival. The links between the health of local publishing and local tech industries appear to be growing in many countries across SSA. Are there any useful models to consider helping meet both objectives—where a country is actively promoting the development of local technology firms and vibrant, competitive local educational publishing markets—while at the same time following textbook procurement practices that are potentially at odds with such goals? In some places, large procurements are broken into many smaller pieces as a way to foster industry development, while at the same time, meeting the more immediate needs for low-cost, high-quality educational content, both digital and traditional.

Partnerships—between international and local educational publishers and between publishers and technology firms—may become increasingly important, and complex. Emerging markets for digital TLM across SSA may be characterized by a combination of partnerships between international publishers, local publishers, and local and international technology firms. The combinations and permutations may be difficult to track as the educational publishing industry comes to a new equilibrium as a result of various technology-enabled disruptions to existing business practices and models. Firms in each of these four quadrants often highlight the importance of having a diverse set of potential partners. If a government considers this sort of thing to be desirable, how might it—and the donor agencies with which it partners—support such linkages as part of its larger effort to ensure that the highest quality educational materials are available in the most accessible ways at the lowest possible cost to learners, both inside its formal education system and outside of it?

In fast-changing markets like those for digital teaching learning materials, care may need to be taken to promote—and not stifle—innovation. Whatever shape or form new activities, policies, and guidelines related to the procurement, production, and usage of TLM might take, countries will need to consider mechanisms that are open to new approaches. Entrenched players with vested interests in maintaining the status quo—publishers, units within government bureaucracies, printing houses, and so forth—may try to protect their interests in the short and medium terms. New actors—technology companies, telecom providers, independent software developers and media firms, and perhaps even user communities of various sorts—may emerge offering innovative products and services that address many of the teaching and learning challenges in ways that complement, extend, or even replace traditional printed textbooks. Where business-as-usual in providing sufficient amounts of affordable, relevant, useful educational resources is not working, countries should consider how a wider variety of groups may be incentivized to explore innovative approaches to the production and distribution of digital TLM—and provide them with the space to do so.

Ten Recommendations for Policymakers

Countries contemplating the use of digital TLM across a country's education system should consider the following 10 general recommendations during the planning processes:

1. **Take a holistic approach.** Countries should not consider investments in digital TLM separately from investments in traditional printed materials. Decisions related to both should be considered in an integrated fashion, and relevant links to related decisions about assessment should be explored as well. A variety of actors, including those outside the education sector not traditionally consulted in matters related to textbook provision in the past, such including the ministry of IT and telecom authority and representatives of the tech industry, should be consulted during policy formulation and decision-making processes.
2. **Pursue complementarity before substitution.** A "big bang" approach to replacing printed textbooks with digital materials on a large scale may be ill-advised. Traditional printed textbooks will continue to be useful tools, and be cost-effective, for many years to come. When investing in digital TLM, first examine how printed and digital materials may complement each other, and concentrate initial investments in digital content in ways that take advantage of affordances or functionalities not offered by traditional printed textbooks.
3. **Assume change (in technologies, in market participants, in content).** The educational publishing industry is undergoing a period of rapid disruption. New players may emerge, and old players may disappear. Digital content produced using "old" standards and technologies may become difficult to support as new technologies and standards emerge. Technological advances may disrupt existing cost structures and business models in fundamental ways. Planners should consider not only how new content will be acquired, but how to ensure seamless transitions during periods of expected change.

4. **Calculate and budget for total costs over time, not just the upfront costs of content acquisition and the purchasing of devices.** Planners should avoid the temptation to focus only on upfront costs of the acquisition of content and the infrastructure necessary to support the distribution and use of this content. Especially where investments in learning materials include investments in technology, estimating total costs over time is critical where the use of these materials needs to be supported over time.
5. **Avoid vendor lock in—and try to ensure a diversity of suppliers and supporting ecosystem or actors and partners.** Lowest cost approaches to the acquisition of digital education content can prove to be very expensive over time if they result in too great a dependence on any one vendor. Lock-in—a situation from which it can be difficult to exit without costly time and expense—can develop on a number of different levels as technology use increases in an education system.
6. **Consider that public relations and community outreach campaigns can be crucial to the adoption of new digital teaching and learning materials.** Simply making available educational content in digital formats may not be sufficient to ensure that it is actually utilized. Providing information to, and enlisting the collaboration and support of, various stakeholder groups—parents, community leaders, teachers, school administrators, civil society groups, and students themselves—can be vital to increase the likelihood that investments in digital TLM are put to productive uses.
7. **Do not neglect training and ongoing support.** Investments in digital TLM may need to be complemented by investments in training, for example for teachers, if such content is to be used successfully across an education system.
8. **New competencies, and possibly even new institutions, may need to be developed to help direct and oversee related activities.** Existing capacity within government may be insufficient to deal with new processes and complexities that typically accompany large-scale investments in digital TLM. New institutions—or new structures within existing institutions—may need to be created and supported to help guide, oversee, and implement efforts to introduce digital educational content. New skill sets may be required for those who have related responsibilities.
9. **Review existing laws and regulations as they may relate to the use of digital teaching and learning materials.** The use of educational content in digital format brings with it a set of new challenges and opportunities related to IP rights. Governments should be prepared to adopt the changes that may be needed to help ensure educational goals and objectives are not compromised as a result of inadequate, outdated, or poorly drafted laws and guidelines.
10. **Assess existing procurement processes to ensure that they are appropriate and relevant—and make changes where necessary.** Existing mechanisms and practices used to procure printed textbooks may not be appropriate, or cost-effective, when procuring learning materials in digital formats. A number of changes in the markets for such content, including the bundling of

various goods and services by vendors, the emergence of "open educational resources," and the need to link or embed digital content within content management or assessment systems may pose challenges to existing procurement processes.

Notes

1. Once adopted at scale, ICTs often long outlive predictions of their permanent demise. It is perhaps worth noting, for example, that the motion picture did not kill radio, just like television did not fully supplant the motion picture. It was only in July 2013 that India, the last country in the world where telegrams were routinely sent—enabled by a technology (the telegraph) first introduced at a large scale in the 1840s in the United States—officially ended its telegraphy service. For more information, see "India Sends Its Last Telegram. Stop," Associated Press, July 15, 2013, http://www.telegraph.co.uk/news/worldnews/asia/india/10180463/India-sends-its-last-telegram.-Stop.html.
2. About 210,000 OLPC laptops have been distributed to students to date in Rwanda, and the government has announced plans to distribute 1 million devices by 2017. For more information, see "Mudasobwa zigera kuri miliyoni zizatangwa muri 'One Laptop per Child' bitarenze 2017" on the Doing Business in Rwanda website, http://www.igihe.com/amakuru/muri-afurika/u-rwanda/mudasobwa-zigera-kuri-miliyoni-zizatangwa-muri-one-laptop-per-child-bitarenze-2017; and the OLPC Rwanda website, http://wiki.laptop.org/go/OLPC_Rwanda.
3. Kenya has announced plans to provide laptops to all primary school students, beginning with a distribution of 450,000 laptops to grade 1 students in 2014. For more information, see Sessional Paper No. 14 of 2012 on Reforming Education and Training Sectors in Kenya (KMHEST 2012); KTN TV, "Education Committee Speaks on Kenya's Laptop Project," http://www.standardmedia.co.ke/ktn/video/watch/2000068804/-education-committee-speaks-on-kenya-s-laptop-project); and Ministry of Education, Science, and Technology, "Laptop Tender Advertisement," http://www.education.go.ke/News.aspx?nid=1876.
4. The lowest cost e-reading device from Amazon, the 6-inch Kindle, holds over 1,000 books. See http://www.amazon.com/dp/B007HCCNJU/ref=sa_menu_kdptq.
5. For more on the Technology Hype Cycle, see http://www.gartner.com/technology/research/methodologies/hype-cycle.jsp.
6. For better or for worse, the use of e-book readers, where text is presented in a static manner that largely conforms to traditional concepts of a "book," often also fits rather comfortably within traditional views of education policymakers related to the delivery and use of education content in schools.
7. For more information on the variety of different costs typically associated with introducing new technologies into educational settings, see "How Much Does It Really Cost to Introduce and Sustain Computers in Schools? Total Cost of Ownership (TCO): A Study of Models of Affordable Computing for Schools in Developing Countries," a discussion sponsored by the EduTech community, http://go.worldbank.org/05HK8LX5U0.
8. The OER Commons is just one of many websites that attempts to catalog, document, and link to such content. See http://www.oercommons.org/.
9. See, for example, Bennett, Matton, and Kervin (2008). This is just one example in a large corpus of scholarly work exploring this topic.

10. Uruguay's ambitious Plan Ceibal has provided free laptops to all primary school students in government schools and is now embarking on distribution to secondary schools as well. See http://www.ceibal.edu.uy/Paginas/Inicio.aspx.
11. However one feels about the value of open education resources, one potential Achilles heel of the "OER movement" is that, while there are lots of groups working on "open content," there are not many organizations developing "open assessment systems."
12. The Flexbook is a content authoring platform offered by the U.S.-based CK-12 Foundation (http://www.ck12.org/student) that enables the aggregation, customization, and repurposing of existing educational content.

References

Bennett, Sue, Karl Matton, and Lisa Kervin. 2008. "The 'Digital Natives' Debate: A Critical Review of the Evidence." *British Journal of Educational Technology* 39 (5): 775–86.

KMHEST (Kenya Ministry of Higher Education, Science and Technology). 2012. *Sessional Paper No. 14 of 2012 on Reforming Education and Training Sectors in Kenya*. Nairobi: KMHEST. http://www.strathmore.edu/pdf/sessional_paper_19th_june_nqf.pdf.

OECD (Organisation for Economic Cooperation and Development). 2009. *Beyond Textbooks: Digital Learning Resources as Systemic Innovation in the Nordic Countries*. Paris: OECD.

Sabarwal, Shwetlena, David Evans, and Anastasia Marshak. 2012. "Textbook Provision and Student Outcomes: The Devil in the Details." Manuscript. World Bank, Washington, DC.

The William and Flora Hewlett Foundation. "Open Educational Resources." Undated. http://www.hewlett.org/programs/education/open-educational-resources.

Trucano, Michael. 2011. "What Happens When All Textbooks Are (Only) Digital? Ask the Koreans!" *EduTech* (blog), July 6. http://blogs.worldbank.org/edutech/korea-digital-textbooks.

CHAPTER 9

Lessons and Recommendations

Factors that affect textbook production in Sub-Saharan Africa (SSA), as well as how these costs might be reduced, are discussed extensively in chapter 5. In particular, a great deal of importance is attached to textbook life. However, longer shelf life, with implicit quality features that impact durability, increases production costs which perpetuates scarcity which, in turn, leads to low textbook use as is observed from anecdotal evidence from all over Africa and is succinctly captured in findings of a Sierra Leone study (Sabarwal, Evans, and Marshak 2012). In developed countries—where textbook availability is universal or close to it—students either buy their books because they can afford to do so or the countries have well-established systems for managing textbooks in schools.

In the United States, for example, most textbooks are expensive, of high quality, and have shelf lives longer than four years. And students receive them for free in public schools, though they (or their parents) must pay for lost or damaged books. Books are given to children from the lower- and upper-secondary grades for the entire school year and collected at the end. Primary students usually receive textbooks to use while in school.

The Philippines follows a similar system in its public schools. Textbook life is estimated to be five years. Children receive books at the start of each year and return them at the end. Loss or damage carries a financial cost to students or their parents. Among developing countries that have succeeded in providing free books to students, India has done so with a textbook:pupil ratio of 1:1 by reducing the shelf life of books to one year. In Vietnam, although the shelf life of textbooks is theoretically four years, 60–70 percent students are expected to buy books and discard or resell them at the end of the school year. Some schools keep the textbooks from the remaining 30–40 percent of students who receive free textbooks. Textbooks are expected to be updated often to keep up with changes to the curriculum. Because parents are responsible for providing updated books, and the government is responsible for providing updated books to children in difficult circumstances and remote locations, the four-year shelf life loses relevance except as an indication of textbook quality and durability.

What then are the most viable options for Sub-Saharan countries to ensure that all children have access to textbooks? With rapid increases in enrollments due to high birthrates, constrained education budgets, and weaknesses in school management, there are no easy answers for immediately achievable results. Though the comparisons with India, the Philippines, and Vietnam offer many lessons—as do experiences from countries across SSA—the option of each child owning a textbook to use or discard at the end of the school year does not appear to be very cost-efficient from a perspective of both production and system costs. Building an inventory of high-quality textbooks with four- to five-year shelf lives, while also cutting costs and improving management and use, seems to be a more viable option. In the longer term, as inventories expand, investments in enhancing shelf life could increase cost efficiency even more. The goal would be to achieve inventories that allow for textbook:pupil ratios of 1:1, with books distributed at the start of the school year and collected at the end, with adequate financing for replenishments and quality enhancements.

How Can Sub-Saharan Countries Lower the High Costs of Providing Textbooks?

The choices available to SSA countries to reduce costs of textbooks and improve textbook provision are provided below. Some SSA countries have already adopted some of the choices described below, but **they must all be adopted simultaneously** as part of larger policy efforts to optimize cost efficiencies. In operationalizing these choices, most countries will face capacity constraints in some or all links in the chain of textbook provision. Thus, the capacity of individual countries would need to be assessed at the level of each link in the chain of textbook provision, and plans to build capacity within a reasonable time frame developed accordingly. This should be possible through external experts working closely with in-house ones to help them become self-reliant in curriculum development, textbook writing, evaluation, and procurement. Depending on the degree of deficiencies in capacity, a graduated approach to capacity building may need to be taken—for example, the focus may be on developing capacity by subsector or by subject areas.

Streamline Curricula
Reducing the number of subjects covered, tightening curriculums to reduce the number of textbooks required, and curtailing their length would significantly lower textbook costs. The median number of textbooks required for grade 1 in the nine SSA countries surveyed for this study is 4 (within a range of 2–9). For grade 6, the median is 7 (range of 7–10). For grade 8, the median is 8 (range of 5–15). And for grade 11, the median is 8 (range of 7–16). The medians for required books at each grade in SSA are higher than the corresponding numbers for India, on par with the Philippines, and lower than for Vietnam. But for many SSA countries the number of textbooks required is very high due to the

large number of subjects in the curriculum. Governments should rationalize curriculums to reduce the number of subjects and, within those, prioritize subjects for textbook provision. They should also sharpen their focus on content to shrink the size of textbooks.

Make Textbooks Conform to Curricula

Many SSA countries still do not have textbooks that reflect their curriculums. It is not an uncommon scenario to have a short list of books evaluated based on their relevance to the curriculum and have such a relationship be as low as 60 percent. Price-based procurement may result in purchase of books that are also low in curriculum relevance. While this ensures cost efficiencies, inefficiencies due to subject coverage are often not weighted. India, the Philippines, and Vietnam have standardized single book policies per subject that conform to their national curriculums. This approach has multiple benefits: it allows for economies of scale, ensures standardization across classrooms, and simplifies textbook upgrading to conform to curriculum revisions. As financing improves, libraries could be used to provide supplemental materials.

Adopt Single Textbook Policies

Decentralized textbook supply systems based on government-approved textbook lists and school-based choices have led many schools in SSA to buy different combinations of textbooks in small numbers for the same subjects and grades. In many countries in the region, this practice was an integral part of school fee abolition policies (as in Ghana, Kenya, Mozambique, Tanzania, and Mozambique). This practice occurred in the Philippines and led to changes to textbook policy. The Department of Education claimed that privatization led to the adoption of multiple titles for a given subject. Thus a school could end up with several different titles for a single subject, at varying costs, without achieving a 1:1 ratio for any one textbook or title. In early 2009, due to similar concerns, Tanzania also sought to address this issue by changing its textbook policy.

The case for choice of textbooks at the school level, exercised by teachers, is weak and impractical in SSA. It is neither cost-effective nor conducive to providing for uniformity across classrooms. A single textbook per subject allows for economies of scale in textbook production and pricing. It also makes it easier to incorporate textbooks in classrooms because all students have access to the same material. In subject areas such as science, mathematics, and languages, countries should explore the possibility of standardizing textbooks through bilateral or multilateral partnerships. Until the 1970s, Kenya, Tanzania, and Uganda shared a curriculum and an examination authority and cross-border trade in textbooks was common. The stated goal of a harmonized school curriculum in the five-member countries of the East African Community, if realized, would provide robust options for textbook development. For culturally neutral subjects such as mathematics, sciences, and technology, it would be economically prudent to borrow, adapt, and translate entire textbook sections or books for different countries.

Strengthen Textbook Development

In his overview of Daniel Tanner's work on U.S. textbooks, Joseph P. Farrell (undated) contends that all governments tend to strongly intervene in textbook development and provision and that there is no such thing as an entirely free market when it comes to textbook provision. Farrel also says that countries differ in their degree, locuses, and mechanisms of state intervention, and in the context to which the state "owns" the various agencies of textbook design, production, and distribution. In some countries, such as the United States, private publishers handle all three of these stages almost exclusively. In other countries, the state presence at all three stages is overwhelming. It is common for the private and public sectors to coexist at one or more of these stages.

SSA countries could adopt one of two new models for developing textbooks. In Ethiopia and the Philippines, textbook development is part of textbook procurement through international competitive bidding. In India and Vietnam, on the other hand, textbooks are developed through subject experts identified by state agencies, and textbooks go through an extensive, well-defined consultation and evaluation processes. The latter approach eliminates the publisher as a middleman, and the government retains copyrights, making reprints cheaper (Farrel). Both approaches ensure conformity with local curriculums but reportedly suffer equally from concerns over quality. Local capacity in textbook writing might need to be developed in SSA. In the interim, textbook development may be bid as part of the publishing package as in Ethiopia and the Philippines. Both models would need to pay adequate attention to ensuring quality, particularly of content.

Make Textbook Printing Competitive

Competitive printing of textbooks cuts their costs. In countries with underdeveloped printing industries, international competitive bidding is a cost-effective option, although the recurrent demand for printing textbooks in large volumes is likely to provide an impetus for expanding local printing capacity.

Improve Textbook Delivery

Textbooks should be delivered to schools quickly and cheaply, and delivery should be part of procurement for printing. Most other approaches adopted by countries have caused delays in distribution due to administrative inefficiencies, lack of funds for transportation, and damage to books from poor storage and handling during transportation. Inevitably the schools in distant, hard-to-reach areas suffer as is evident from the discrepancies in the student:textbook ratios between rural and urban areas in most parts of the developing world (Montagnes 2000).

Expand Infrastructure and Address School-Level Management Deficiencies

Safe storage for textbooks is required whether students initially share books through libraries or are able to keep them until the end of the school year. Thus libraries should be a priority in efforts to strengthen school infrastructure.

Textbook provision is often seen as an end in itself—even by donors—with little emphasis placed on their use by students and teachers.

Thus systems should ensure that textbooks have to be used and that students have easy access to them. The first goal would require regular use of textbooks in classrooms by teachers, homework that requires the use of textbooks and other teaching and learning materials, group assignments using textbooks, and the like. The second would include giving textbooks to students on a rotating or sharing basis, providing space in libraries for students to work on individual and group assignments, and encouraging accountability for book safety, maintenance, and storage. In an atmosphere of low textbook use by teachers and weak school management, good textbook management poses a major challenge. To overcome this, use of textbooks and other teaching and learning materials and the management of such must be an integral part of all school management and preservice and in-service teacher training.

Secure Sustainable, Predictable Financing

Sustainable, predictable budget allocations for textbooks are essential to adequate textbook provision. Countries need to plan for targeted provision of textbooks and other learning materials at the primary and secondary levels with estimates of the funding required as well as supporting timeframes to meet and maintain the targets. Countries might need to rely on external funding to build their initial textbook inventories. But protected budget allocations should be set and maintained to ensure sustained textbook supplies.

If countries put in place the systems required to address the factors causing unaffordable textbook costs, funding shortages should not be a binding constraint on ensuring that all students in SSA have access to textbooks. Based on education budgets and student enrollments in 31 SSA countries and reasonable assumptions about unit costs and book lives, spending 3–5 percent of the primary education budget on textbooks should allow a country to provide all pupils with three to five textbooks per grade. To that should be added 1–2 percent of the budget to achieve a minimum provision of other teaching and learning materials.

Similarly, based on budgets and enrollments in 29 SSA countries and reasonable assumptions about unit and system costs, spending 4–6 percent of the secondary education budget on textbooks would allow the median country to provide all pupils with five to eight textbooks per grade if unit costs can be lowered US$5. If a five-year textbook life can be achieved, a budget allocation of about 6 percent would permit providing eight books to all students at a unit book price of US$8.

Exercise Caution in Large-Scale Adoption of Technology

The infiltration of technology in education is inevitable. There has been a strong buzz about electronic readers. Similarly, Kenya has taken the ambitious plunge of providing a laptop to each student. Though technology will clearly play an increasing role in education, this role will depend on the absorptive capacity of local systems and the availability of supporting infrastructure—and, of course, financial resources.

Scarce resources require judicious choices. Other resources should supplement textbooks to enhance learning. Visual and electronic media play an important role in this regard and need to be carefully targeted at students as well as teachers to derive their biggest benefits. Investments in enabling infrastructure are critical to harness technology for learning and before making any decisions about introducing technology in education. An assessment of the costs associated with technology, fixed and recurrent, is essential. Meanwhile, the choices are neither simple nor cost-efficient, and in SSA, there is no viable substitute for the traditional textbooks in the near term.

References

Farrell, Joseph P. Undated. "Overview, School Textbooks in the United States." *Education Encyclopedia* (online resource). http://education.stateuniversity.com/pages/2507/Textbooks.html.

Montagnes, Ian. 2000. *Textbooks and Learning Materials 1990–1999: A Global Survey*. Paris: UNESCO.

Sabarwal, Shwetlena, David Evans, and Anastasia Marshak. 2012. "Textbook Provision and Student Outcomes: The Devil in the Details." Manuscript. World Bank, Washington, DC.

Environmental Benefits Statement

The World Bank Group is committed to reducing its environmental footprint. In support of this commitment, the Publishing and Knowledge Division leverages electronic publishing options and print-on-demand technology, which is located in regional hubs worldwide. Together, these initiatives enable print runs to be lowered and shipping distances decreased, resulting in reduced paper consumption, chemical use, greenhouse gas emissions, and waste.

The Publishing and Knowledge Division follows the recommended standards for paper use set by the Green Press Initiative. Whenever possible, books are printed on 50 percent to 100 percent postconsumer recycled paper, and at least 50 percent of the fiber in our book paper is either unbleached or bleached using Totally Chlorine Free (TCF), Processed Chlorine Free (PCF), or Enhanced Elemental Chlorine Free (EECF) processes.

More information about the Bank's environmental philosophy can be found at http://crinfo.worldbank.org/wbcrinfo/node/4.

www.ingramcontent.com/pod-product-compliance
Lightning Source LLC
Chambersburg PA
CBHW082126230426
43671CB00015B/2822